# UK TOWER AIR FRYER
# COOKBOOK
# WITH COLOUR PICTURES

1800 Days Quick, Delicious Air Fryer Recipes for Beginners and Pros. for Perfect Frying Incl.Tips and Tricks| UK Measurements & UK Ingredients

**Mark Anderson**

## Legal & Disclaimer

The content and information in this book is consistent and truthful, and it has been provided for informational, educational and business purposes only.

The illustrations in the book are from the website shutterstock.com, depositphoto.com and freepik.com and have been authorized.

The content and information contained in this book has been compiled from reliable sources, which are accurate based on the knowledge, belief, expertise and information of the Author. The author cannot be held liable for any omissions and/or errors.

# TABLE OF
# CONTENT

# INTRODUCTION

Greetings, fellow culinary explorers! In the pages that follow, I'm excited to invite you into a world where delectable flavours and wholesome choices come together in perfect harmony—all thanks to the remarkable Tower Air Fryer. This isn't just a cookbook; it's an invitation to a healthier way of cooking and savouring your favorite dishes.

Picture this: crispy, golden-brown exteriors that crunch at the slightest touch, revealing succulent interiors bursting with flavour. Now, imagine achieving this culinary magic with a fraction of the oil traditionally required. That's the promise of the Tower Air Fryer. As we dive into these recipes, you'll discover how this ingenious appliance empowers us to indulge in the satisfying textures and tastes of fried dishes, while still honouring our health-conscious aspirations.

Air frying isn't just a trend—it's a culinary revolution that has taken kitchens by storm. As we evolve our approach to cooking, embracing innovative methods that align with our well-being becomes paramount. Air frying has not only won over our taste buds but has also ushered in a new era of cooking that resonates with the modern lifestyle. We're embracing a method that delights in both flavours and nutrients, and the Tower Air Fryer is at the forefront of this exciting change.

Here's where our culinary journey takes a turn into tantalizing territory. The recipes you'll find within these pages are specially crafted to harness the full potential of the Tower Air Fryer. Each dish is a testament to the appliance's ability to deliver crispy perfection without compromising on health. Whether you're a novice or a seasoned home cook, this cookbook aims to be your go-to guide for creating mouthwatering meals that celebrate flavour, wellness, and the joys of cooking.

So, as we embark on this adventure together, armed with the Tower Air Fryer and a passion for vibrant cooking, let's savour every moment in the kitchen. Let's create dishes that not only nourish our bodies but also elevate our senses. With every recipe, let's revel in the delightful intersection of wholesome and irresistible. Here's to embracing a healthier culinary journey that's as exciting as it is delicious.

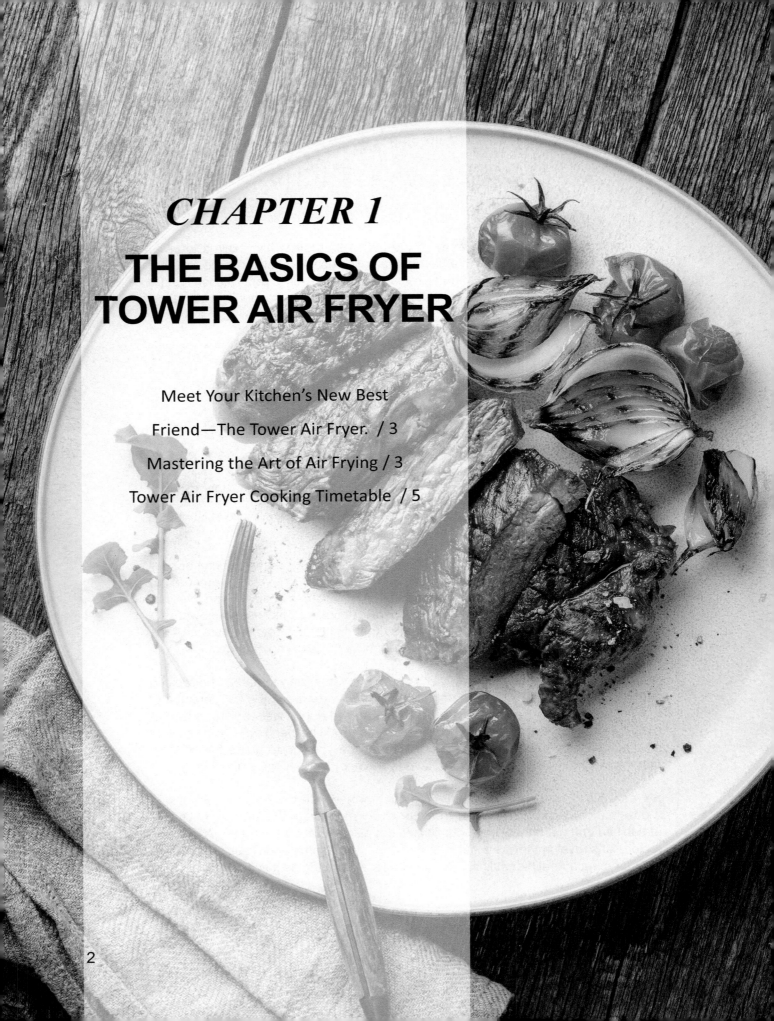

# CHAPTER 1
# THE BASICS OF TOWER AIR FRYER

Welcome to the heart of our air frying adventure, where we'll unravel the fundamentals of making magic happen with the Tower Air Fryer. This chapter is all about laying the foundation for your culinary journey, ensuring you're armed with the knowledge and skills to create crispy, flavourful dishes that are as healthy as they are satisfying.

## Meet Your Kitchen's New Best Friend—The Tower Air Fryer.

This remarkable appliance boasts a design that combines innovation and convenience, allowing you to create dishes that are beautifully golden on the outside and tender on the inside. Its sleek structure houses a rapid air circulation system, ensuring that heat is evenly distributed for consistent results.

At first, please see the structure of Tower Air Fryer as follow:

1. Working light
2. Power light
3. Timer dial
4. Temperature dial
5. Air inlet
6. Air outlet
7. Basket
8. Basket handle
9. Basket release button

Let's dive into the magic of air frying. It's a cooking method that revolves around circulating hot air around your ingredients, creating that irresistible crispy texture we all adore. What sets the Tower apart is its ability to achieve this with a fraction of the oil you'd traditionally use. Imagine indulging in the guilty pleasures of fried food while keeping your health goals in check. That's the power of air frying, and the Tower Air Fryer is your trusty accomplice on this flavourful journey.

Gone are the days of drenching your dishes in oil for that perfect crunch. With the Tower Air Fryer, you're embracing a healthier way of cooking that doesn't compromise on taste. By using minimal oil or even none at all, you're reducing calorie intake while preserving the nutritional integrity of your ingredients. Think of it as a culinary win-win—a way to enjoy the flavours you love without the guilt.

## Mastering the Art of Air Frying

Now that you're acquainted with the Tower's prowess, let's get into the nitty-gritty of using it like a pro. Preheating is your first step towards culinary success—ensuring that the hot air starts working its magic from the moment your ingredients hit the fryer basket. As for cooking times and temperatures, they're your secret weapons for achieving that perfect balance between crispiness and succulence.

**Preheatings:**

If you want to preheat the appliance before cooking. turn the timer dial to a time higher than 3 minutes and wait until the heating-up light goes out. Then fill the basket and turn the timer dial to the required preparation time.

**Setting Cooking Times:**

Timing is everything in air frying. Most recipes will guide you on cooking times, but it's always wise to keep an eye on your food. Remember that the Tower Air Fryer's rapid air circulation speeds up the process, so a few minutes can make a big difference. It's a dance between flavours and textures, so be vigilant!

The Air Fryer has a 60 minute manual timer with a bell. Turn the dial to set the required cooking time. When the cooking time has elapsed, a bell will sound to indicate that cooking has finished.

**Shaking or Flipping:**

Depending on the recipe, you might need to shake the basket or flip the ingredients halfway through cooking for even browning. Remember to follow your recipe's instructions. To shake the ingredients, pull the pan out of the appliance by the handle and shake it. Then slide the pan back into the fryer. Caution: Be careful not to press the basket release button on the handle while shaking your ingredients.

If you set the timer to half the preparation time, the timer bell will sound to indicate when you have to shake the ingredients. However, this means that you have to set the timer again to the remaining preparation time after shaking.

**Proper Use and Care:**

Our Tower Air Fryer is a kitchen superhero, but even superheroes need care. Always use utensils that are safe for non-stick surfaces to avoid damaging the fryer basket. And remember, even though it uses minimal oil, a little goes a long way. Lightly coat your ingredients for that perfect crispness.

So, armed with the knowledge of preheating, temperatures, and cooking times, you're well on your way to air frying mastery. As we move forward, be prepared to delve into a world of flavour and creativity, where the Tower Air Fryer's capabilities are your palette and your dishes are the masterpieces. Let's dive in!

# Tower Air Fryer Cooking Timetable

| Food Type | Min – Max (g) | Time (min) | Temp (°C) | Shake | Remark |
|---|---|---|---|---|---|
| **Potato & fries** | | | | | |
| Thin frozen fries | 400-500 | 18-20 | 200 | shake | |
| Thick frozen fries | 400-500 | 20-25 | 200 | shake | |
| Potato gratin | 600 | 20-25 | 200 | shake | |
| **Meat & Poultry** | | | | | |
| Steak | 100-600 | 10-15 | 180 | | |
| Pork chops | 100-600 | 10-15 | 180 | | |
| Hamburger | 100-600 | 10-15 | 180 | | |
| Sausage roll | 100-600 | 13-15 | 200 | | |
| Drumsticks | 100-600 | 25-30 | 180 | | |
| Chicken breast | 100-600 | 15-20 | 180 | | |
| **Snacks** | | | | | |
| Spring rolls | 100-500 | 8-10 | 200 | shake | Use oven-ready |
| Frozen chicken nuggets | 100-600 | 6-10 | 200 | shake | Use oven-ready |
| Frozen fish fingers | 100-500 | 6-10 | 200 | Use oven-ready | |
| Frozen bread crumbed cheese snacks | 100-500 | 8-10 | 180 | Use oven-ready | |
| Stuffed vegetables | 100-500 | 10 | 160 | | |
| **Baking** | | | | | |
| Cake | 400 | 20-25 | 160 | Use baking tin | |
| Quiche | 500 | 20-22 | 180 | Use baking tin/oven dish | |
| Muffins | 400 | 15-18 | 200 | Use baking tin | |
| Sweet snacks | 500 | 20 | 160 | Use baking tin/oven dish | |

# CHAPTER 2
# BREAKFAST

# Tofu with Mushroom Omelette

SERVES 2

PREP TIME: 15 minutes
COOK TIME: 28 minutes

¼ of onion, chopped
230 g silken tofu, pressed and sliced
100 g fresh mushrooms, sliced
3 eggs, beaten
30 ml milk
**What you'll need from the store cupboard:**
10 ml rapeseed oil
1 garlic clove, minced
Salt and black pepper, to taste

1. Preheat the Air fryer to 180°C and grease an Air Fryer pan.
2. Heat oil in the Air Fryer pan and add garlic and onion.
3. Bake for about 3 minutes and stir in the tofu and mushrooms.
4. Season with salt and black pepper and top with the beaten eggs.
5. Bake for about 25 minutes, poking the eggs twice in between.
6. Dish out and serve warm.

# Streaky Rasher and Hot Dog Omelette

SERVES 2

PREP TIME: 10 minutes
COOK TIME: 10 minutes

4 eggs
1 streaky rasher, chopped
2 hot dogs, chopped
2 small onions, chopped
2 tbsps. milk
**What you'll need from the store cupboard:**
Salt and black pepper, to taste

1. Preheat the Air fryer to 165°C and grease an Air Fryer pan.
2. Whisk together eggs and stir in the remaining ingredients.
3. Stir well to combine and place in the Air fryer.
4. Bake for about 10 minutes and serve hot.

# Spinach with Egg Cups

**SERVES 4**

PREP TIME: 15 minutes
COOK TIME: 23 minutes

**15 g unsalted butter, melted**
**450 g fresh baby spinach**
**4 eggs**
**200 g gammon, sliced**
**4 tsps. milk**
**What you'll need from the store cupboard:**
**15 ml olive oil**
**Salt and black pepper, to taste**

1. Preheat the Air fryer at 185°C and grease 4 ramekins with butter.
2. Heat olive oil in a pan and add spinach.
3. Sauté for about 3 minutes and drain the liquid completely from the spinach.
4. Divide the spinach equally into the prepared ramekins and add gammon slices.
5. Crack 1 egg over gammon in each ramekin and pour milk evenly over eggs.
6. Season with salt and black pepper and transfer the ramekins in the Air fryer.
7. Bake for about 20 minutes and serve warm.

# Chicken and Broccoli Quiche

**SERVES 8**

PREP TIME: 15 minutes
COOK TIME: 12 minutes

**1 frozen ready-made shortcrust pastry**
**1 egg**
**30 g cheddar cheese, grated**
**18 g boiled broccoli, chopped**
**50 g cooked chicken, chopped**
**What you'll need from the store cupboard:**
**½ tbsp. olive oil**
**45 ml double cream**
**Salt and black pepper, to taste**

1. Preheat the Air fryer to 200°C and grease 2 small pie pans with olive oil.
2. Whisk egg with double cream, cheese, salt and black pepper in a bowl.
3. Cut 2 (13-centimetre) rounds from the shortcrust pastry and arrange in each pie pan.
4. Press in the bottom and sides gently and pour the egg mixture over pie crust.
5. Top evenly with chicken and broccoli and place the pie pans into an Air Fryer basket.
6. Bake for about 12 minutes and dish out to serve hot.

# Healthy Courgette Fritters

**SERVES 4**

PREP TIME: 15 minutes
COOK TIME: 7 minutes

35 g plain flour
2 eggs
300 g courgette, grated and squeezed
200 g Halloumi cheese
1 tsp. fresh dill, minced
**What you'll need from the store cupboard:**
Salt and black pepper, to taste

1. Preheat the Air fryer to 180°C and grease a baking dish.
2. Mix together all the ingredients in a large bowl.
3. Make small fritters from this mixture and place them on the prepared baking dish.
4. Transfer the dish in the Air Fryer basket and bake for about 7 minutes.
5. Dish out and serve warm.

# Mini Tomato Quiche

**SERVES 2**

PREP TIME: 15 minutes
COOK TIME: 30 minutes

120 ml milk
115 g Gouda cheese, shredded
4 eggs
30 g onion, chopped
100 g tomatoes, chopped
**What you'll need from the store cupboard:**
Salt, to taste

1. Preheat the Air fryer to 170°C and grease a large ramekin with cooking spray.
2. Mix together all the ingredients in a ramekin and transfer into the air fryer basket.
3. Bake for about 30 minutes and dish out to serve hot.

# Pumpkin with Yoghurt Bread

**SERVES 4**

**PREP TIME:** 10 minutes
**COOK TIME:** 15 minutes

4 tbsps. plain Greek yoghurt
6 tbsps. porridge oats
2 large eggs
8 tbsps. pumpkin puree
6 tbsps. banana flour
**What you'll need from the store cupboard:**
4 tbsps. honey
2 tbsps. vanilla essence
Pinch of ground nutmeg

1. Preheat the Air fryer to 180°C and grease a loaf pan.
2. Mix together all the ingredients except oats in a bowl and beat with the hand mixer until smooth.
3. Add oats and mix until well combined.
4. Transfer the mixture into the prepared loaf pan and place in the Air fryer.
5. Bake for about 15 minutes and remove from the Air fryer.
6. Place onto a wire rack to cool and cut the bread into desired size slices to serve.

# Mushroom with Tomato Frittata

**SERVES 2**

**PREP TIME:** 15 minutes
**COOK TIME:** 14 minutes

3 eggs
6 fresh mushrooms, sliced
1 streaky rasher, chopped
6 cherry tomatoes, halved
50 g fresh baby spinach
115 g Parmesan cheese, grated
**What you'll need from the store cupboard:**
15 ml olive oil
Salt and black pepper, to taste

1. Preheat the Air fryer to 200°C and grease a baking dish lightly.
2. Mix together streaky rasher, mushrooms, tomatoes, salt and black pepper in the baking dish.
3. Arrange the baking dish into the Air Fryer basket and bake for about 6 minutes.
4. Whisk together eggs in a small bowl and add cheese.
5. Mix well and pour over the streaky rasher mixture.
6. Place the baking dish in the Air Fryer basket and bake for about 8 minutes.
7. Dish out and serve hot.

# Eggs, Mushrooms with Tomato Scramble

**SERVES 4**

| | |
|---|---|
| PREP TIME: 15 minutes<br>COOK TIME: 11 minutes | 1 tbsp. chives, chopped<br>180 ml milk<br>4 eggs<br>8 grape tomatoes, halved<br>35 g mushrooms, sliced<br>**What you'll need from the store cupboard:**<br>Salt and black pepper, to taste |

1. Preheat the Air fryer to 180°C and grease an Air Fryer pan.
2. Whisk eggs with milk, salt, and black pepper in a bowl.
3. Transfer the egg mixture into the Air Fryer pan and bake for about 6 minutes.
4. Add mushrooms, grape tomatoes and chives and bake for about 5 minutes.
5. Dish out and serve warm.

# Pak Choi with Egg Frittata

**SERVES 2**

| | |
|---|---|
| PREP TIME: 15 minutes<br>COOK TIME: 8 minutes | 70 g pak choi, chopped<br>2 eggs<br>30 ml milk<br>7 g cheddar cheese, grated<br>7 g feta cheese, grated<br>**What you'll need from the store cupboard:**<br>Salt and black pepper, to taste<br>15 ml olive oil<br>Cooking spray |

1. Preheat the Air fryer to 180°C and grease an Air Fryer pan with cooking spray.
2. Whisk together eggs with milk, salt and black pepper in a bowl.
3. Heat olive oil in the Air Fryer pan and add pak choi.
4. Bake for about 3 minutes and stir in the whisked eggs.
5. Top with cheddar and feta cheese and bake for about 5 minutes.
6. Dish out and serve hot.

# Chicken Omelette

**SERVES 8**

| | |
|---|---|
| PREP TIME: 15 minutes<br>COOK TIME: 16 minutes | ½ red chilli, seeded and chopped<br>3 eggs<br>1 tsp. butter<br>1 onion, chopped<br>50 g chicken, cooked and shredded<br>**What you'll need from the store cupboard:**<br>Salt and black pepper, to taste |

1. Preheat the Air fryer to 180°C and grease an Air Fryer pan.
2. Heat butter in a frying pan over medium heat and add onions.
3. Sauté for about 5 minutes and add red chilli.
4. Sauté for about 1 minute and stir in the chicken.
5. Remove from the heat and keep aside.
6. Meanwhile, whisk together the eggs, salt, and black pepper in a bowl.
7. Place the chicken mixture into the prepared pan and top with the egg mixture.
8. Bake for about 10 minutes until completely done and serve hot.

# Breakfast Courgette

| PREP TIME: 5 minutes<br>COOK TIME: 25 minutes | 2 small pepper, chopped medium<br>2 small onion, chopped medium<br>4 courgettes, diced into 2-centimetre pieces, drained<br>**What you'll need from the store cupboard:**<br>Cooking oil spray<br>Pinch salt and black pepper |
| --- | --- |

1. Preheat the Air fryer to 175°C and grease the Air fryer basket with cooking spray.
2. Season the courgette with salt and black pepper and place in the Air fryer basket.
3. Select Roasting mode and bake for about 20 minutes, stirring occasionally.
4. Add onion and pepper and roast for 5 more minutes.
5. Remove from the Air fryer and mix well to serve warm.

# Sausage Frittata

SERVES 2

| PREP TIME: 15 minutes<br>COOK TIME: 11 minutes | 3 jumbo eggs<br>30 g feta cheese, crumbled<br>½ of chorizo sausage, sliced<br>85 g frozen corn<br>1 large potato, boiled, peeled and cubed<br>**What you'll need from the store cupboard:**<br>15 ml olive oil<br>Salt and black pepper, to taste |
| --- | --- |

1. Preheat the Air fryer to 180°C and grease an Air Fryer pan.
2. Whisk together eggs with salt and black pepper in a bowl.
3. Heat olive oil in the Air Fryer pan and add sausage, corn and potato.
4. Bake for about 6 minutes and stir in the whisked eggs.
5. Top with cheese and bake for about 5 minutes.
6. Dish out and serve hot.

# Delicious Trout Frittata

SERVES 4

| PREP TIME: 15 minutes<br>COOK TIME: 23 minutes | 4 g fresh dill, chopped<br>1 tomato, chopped<br>1 onion, sliced<br>6 eggs<br>2 hot-smoked trout fillets, chopped<br>**What you'll need from the store cupboard:**<br>60 ml olive oil<br>½ tbsp. horseradish sauce<br>2 tbsps. crème fraiche |
| --- | --- |

1. Preheat the Air fryer to 165°C and grease a baking dish lightly.
2. Whisk together eggs with horseradish sauce and crème fraiche in a bowl.
3. Heat olive oil in a pan and add onions.
4. Sauté for about 3 minutes and transfer into a baking dish.
5. Stir in the whisked eggs, trout, tomato and dill.
6. Arrange the baking dish into an air fryer basket and bake for about 20 minutes.
7. Dish out and serve hot.

# CHAPTER 3
# VEGETABLES

# Easy Glazed Carrots

**PREP TIME:** 10 minutes
**COOK TIME:** 12 minutes

225 g carrots, peeled and cut into large chunks
**What you'll need from the store cupboard:**
15 ml olive oil
20 g honey
Salt and black pepper, to taste

1. Preheat the Air fryer to 200°C and grease an Air fryer basket.
2. Mix all the ingredients in a bowl and toss to coat well.
3. Transfer into the Air fryer basket and bake for about 12 minutes.
4. Dish out and serve hot.

# Crispy Bacon Wrapped Asparagus Bundles

**PREP TIME:** 20 minutes
**COOK TIME:** 8 minutes

4 streaky rashers
½ tbsp. sesame seeds, toasted
450 g asparagus
**What you'll need from the store cupboard:**
1 garlic clove, minced
1 tbsps. brown sugar
20 ml olive oil
½ tbsp. sesame oil, toasted

1. Preheat the Air fryer to 180°C and grease an Air fryer basket.
2. Mix garlic, brown sugar, olive oil and sesame oil in a bowl till sugar is dissolved.
3. Divide asparagus into 4 equal bunches and wrap a streaky rasher slice around each bunch.
4. Rub the asparagus bunch with garlic mixture and arrange in the Air fryer basket.
5. Sprinkle with sesame seeds and bake for about 8 minutes.
6. Dish out and serve hot.

# Super Crispy Tofu

PREP TIME: 15 minutes
COOK TIME: 30 minutes

**340 g extra-firm tofu, drained and cubed into 2.5-centimetre size**
**1 tsp. butter**
**1 chicken stock cube, crushed**
**What you'll need from the store cupboard:**
**2 tbsps. low-sodium soy sauce**
**2 tbsps. fish sauce**
**1 tsp. sesame oil**

1. Preheat the Air fryer to 180°C and grease an Air fryer basket.
2. Mix soy sauce, fish sauce, sesame oil and crushed chicken stock cube in a bowl and toss to coat well.
3. Stir in the tofu cubes and mix until well combined.
4. Keep aside to marinate for about 30 minutes and then transfer into Air fryer basket.
5. Roast for about 30 minutes, flipping every 10 minutes and serve hot.

# Refreshing Broccoli

PREP TIME: 10 minutes
COOK TIME: 21 minutes

**1 tbsp. white sesame seeds**
**30 ml vegetable stock**
**15 g butter**
**1 large head broccoli, cut into bite-sized pieces**
**What you'll need from the store cupboard:**
**15 ml fresh lemon juice**
**3 garlic cloves, chopped**
**½ tsp. fresh lemon zest, grated finely**
**½ tsp. red pepper flakes, crushed**

1. Preheat the Air fryer to 180°C and grease an Air fryer pan.
2. Mix butter, vegetable stock and lemon juice in the Air fryer pan.
3. Transfer into the Air fryer and bake for about 2 minutes.
4. Stir in garlic and broccoli and bake for about 14 minutes.
5. Add sesame seeds, lemon zest and red pepper flakes and bake for 5 minutes.
6. Dish out and serve warm.

# Perfectly Roasted Mushrooms

**SERVES 4**

**PREP TIME:** 10 minutes
**COOK TIME:** 32 minutes

**30 ml white vermouth**
**15 g butter**
**900 g mushrooms, quartered**
**What you'll need from the store cupboard:**
**2 tsps. herbs de Provence**
**½ tsp. garlic powder**

1. Preheat the Air fryer to 160°C and grease an Air fryer pan.
2. Mix herbs de Provence, garlic powder and butter in the Air fryer pan and transfer into the Air fryer basket.
3. Grill for about 2 minutes and stir in the mushrooms.
4. Grill for about 25 minutes and add white vermouth.
5. Grill for 5 more minutes and dish out to serve warm.

# Easy Baked Vegetables

**SERVES 4**

**PREP TIME:** 10 minutes
**COOK TIME:** 35 minutes

**1 tbsp. tarragon leaves, chopped**
**230 g carrots, peeled and sliced**
**450 g yellow marrow, sliced**
**450 g courgette, sliced**
**150 g asparagus**
**What you'll need from the store cupboard:**
**30 ml olive oil, divided**
**1 tsp. kosher salt**
**½ tsp. ground white pepper**

1. Preheat the Air fryer to 200°C and grease an Air fryer basket.
2. Mix 10 ml olive oil and carrots in a bowl until combined.
3. Transfer into the Air fryer basket and bake for about 5 minutes.
4. Meanwhile, mix remaining 20 ml of olive oil, yellow marrow, courgette, salt and white pepper in a large bowl.
5. Transfer this veggie mixture into the Air fryer basket with carrots.
6. Bake for about 30 minutes and dish out in a bowl.
7. Top with tarragon leaves and mix well to serve.

# Cheesy Mushrooms

**SERVES 4**

PREP TIME: 10 minutes
COOK TIME: 8 minutes

**15 g cheddar cheese, grated**
**170 g button mushrooms, stemmed**
**15 g mozzarella cheese, grated**
**What you'll need from the store cupboard:**
**1 tsp. dried dill**
**60 ml olive oil**
**2 tbsps. Italian dried mixed herbs**
**Salt and freshly ground black pepper, to taste**

1. Preheat the Air fryer to 180°C and grease an Air fryer basket.
2. Mix mushrooms, Italian dried mixed herbs, oil, salt and black pepper in a bowl and toss to coat well.
3. Arrange the mushrooms in the Air fryer basket and top with mozzarella cheese and cheddar cheese.
4. Bake for about 8 minutes and sprinkle with dried dill to serve.

# Caramelized Brussels Sprout

**SERVES 4**

PREP TIME: 10 minutes
COOK TIME: 35 minutes

**20 g butter, melted**
**450 g Brussels sprouts, trimmed and halved**
**What you'll need from the store cupboard:**
**Salt and black pepper, to taste**

1. Preheat the Air fryer to 200°C and grease an Air fryer basket.
2. Mix all the ingredients in a bowl and toss to coat well.
3. Arrange the Brussels sprouts in the Air fryer basket and grill for about 35 minutes.
4. Dish out and serve warm.

# Family Favourite Potatoes

| PREP TIME: 10 minutes<br>COOK TIME: 20 minutes | 170 g Greek plain yoghurt<br>340 g waxy potatoes, cubed and boiled<br>**What you'll need from the store cupboard:**<br>60 ml olive oil, divided<br>1 tbsp. paprika, divided<br>Salt and black pepper, to taste |
|---|---|

1. Preheat the Air fryer to 180°C and grease an Air fryer basket.
2. Mix 15 ml olive oil, 1/3 tbsp. of paprika and black pepper in a bowl and toss with potatoes to coat well.
3. Transfer into the Air fryer basket and bake for about 20 minutes.
4. Mix yoghurt, remaining oil, salt and black pepper in a bowl and serve with potatoes.

# Radish with Mozzarella Salad

| PREP TIME: 15 minutes<br>COOK TIME: 30 minutes | 680 g radishes, trimmed and halved<br>230 g fresh mozzarella, sliced<br>**What you'll need from the store cupboard:**<br>Salt and freshly ground black pepper, to taste<br>45 ml olive oil<br>1 tsp. honey |
|---|---|

1. Preheat the Air fryer to 175°C and grease an Air fryer basket with olive oil.
2. Mix radishes, mozzarella, salt, black pepper and 30 ml of olive oil in a bowl and toss to coat well.
3. Arrange the radishes mixture in the Air fryer basket and bake for about 30 minutes, flipping twice in between.
4. Dish out in a bowl and top with the remaining ingredients to serve.

# Cold Salad and Pasta and Veggies

| PREP TIME: 30 minutes<br>COOK TIME: 1 hour 35 minutes | 4 medium tomatoes, cut in eighths<br>1½ kg cooked pasta<br>3 medium courgettes, sliced into 1-centimetre thick rounds<br>3 small aubergines, sliced into 1-centimetre rounds<br>70 g Parmesan cheese, grated<br>**What you'll need from the store cupboard:**<br>60 ml olive oil, divided<br>115 ml fat-free Italian dressing<br>Salt, to taste |
|---|---|

1. Preheat the Air fryer to 180°C and grease an Air fryer basket.
2. Mix courgette and 15 ml of olive oil in a bowl and toss to coat well.
3. Arrange the courgette slices in the Air fryer basket and bake for about 25 minutes.
4. Mix aubergines and 15 ml of olive oil in another bowl and toss to coat well.
5. Arrange the aubergine slices in the Air fryer basket and bake for about 40 minutes.
6. Set the Air fryer to 160°C and place tomatoes into the prepared basket.
7. Bake for about 30 minutes and combine all the Air fried vegetables.
8. Stir in the remaining ingredients and refrigerate covered for at least 2 hours to serve.

# Veggie-filled Pumpkin Basket

**SERVES 6**

| | |
|---|---|
| **PREP TIME:** 15 minutes<br>**COOK TIME:** 30 minutes | **1 onion, chopped**<br>**1 pumpkin, seeded**<br>**1 sweet potato, peeled and chopped**<br>**1 parsnip, peeled and chopped**<br>**70 g peas, shelled**<br>**What you'll need from the store cupboard:**<br>**2 garlic cloves, minced**<br>**2 tsps. herb mix** |

1. Preheat the Air fryer to 180°C and grease an Air fryer basket.
2. Mix all the ingredients in a bowl except pumpkin and toss to coat well.
3. Stuff the vegetable mixture half way into the pumpkin and transfer into the Air fryer basket.
4. Bake for about 30 minutes and dish out to serve warm.

# Garden Fresh Veggie Medley

**SERVES 4**

| | |
|---|---|
| **PREP TIME:** 10 minutes<br>**COOK TIME:** 15 minutes | **3 tomatoes, chopped**<br>**2 small onions, chopped**<br>**2 yellow peppers, seeded and chopped**<br>**1 aubergine, chopped**<br>**1 courgette, chopped**<br>**What you'll need from the store cupboard:**<br>**2 garlic cloves, minced**<br>**2 tbsps. herbs de Provence**<br>**15 ml olive oil**<br>**15 ml balsamic vinegar**<br>**Salt and black pepper, to taste** |

1. Preheat the Air fryer to 180°C and grease an Air fryer basket.
2. Mix all the ingredients in a bowl and toss to coat well.
3. Transfer into the Air fryer basket and grill for about 15 minutes.
4. Keep in the Air fryer for about 5 minutes and dish out to serve hot.

# Chewy Glazed Parsnips

**SERVES 6**

| | |
|---|---|
| **PREP TIME:** 10 minutes<br>**COOK TIME:** 44 minutes | **900 g parsnips, peeled and cut into 2.5-centimetre chunks**<br>**15 g butter, melted**<br>**What you'll need from the store cupboard:**<br>**¼ tsp. red pepper flakes, crushed**<br>**30 ml maple syrup**<br>**1 tbsp. dried parsley flakes, crushed** |

1. Preheat the Air fryer to 180°C and grease an Air fryer basket.
2. Mix parsnips and butter in a bowl and toss to coat well.
3. Arrange the parsnips in the Air fryer basket and bake for about 40 minutes.
4. Meanwhile, mix remaining ingredients in a large bowl.
5. Transfer this mixture into the Air fryer basket and bake for about 4 more minutes.
6. Dish out and serve warm.

# CHAPTER 4
# FISH AND SEAFOOD

# Garlic with Lemon Tilapia

**SERVES 4**

PREP TIME: 5 minutes
COOK TIME: 10 to 15 minutes

**1 tsp. minced garlic**
**½ tsp. chilli powder**
**1 tbsp. lemon juice**
**1 tbsp. olive oil**
**4 (170-g) tilapia fillets**
**10 g spinach, for garnish**

1. Preheat the air fryer to 190ºC. Line the air fryer basket with parchment paper.
2. In a large, shallow bowl, mix together the lemon juice, olive oil, garlic, and chilli powder to make a marinade. Place the tilapia fillets in the bowl and coat evenly.
3. Place the fillets in the basket in a single layer, leaving space between each fillet. You may need to cook in more than one batch.
4. Air fry until the fish is cooked and flakes easily with a fork, 10 to 15 minutes.
5. Serve hot.

# Easy Salmon Bites

**SERVES 4**

PREP TIME: 15 minutes
COOK TIME: 10 to 15 minutes

**2 tbsps. parsley flakes**
**2 tsps. Old Bay seasoning**
**Cooking spray**
**4 (142-g) tins pink salmon, skinless, boneless in water, drained**
**2 eggs, beaten**
**125 g whole-wheat panko bread crumbs**
**4 tbsps. finely minced red pepper**

1. Preheat the air fryer to 180ºC.
2. Spray the air fryer basket lightly with cooking spray.
3. In a medium bowl, mix the salmon, eggs, panko bread crumbs, red pepper, parsley flakes, and Old Bay seasoning.
4. Using a small cookie scoop, form the mixture into 20 balls.
5. Place the salmon bites in the air fryer basket in a single layer and spray lightly with cooking spray. You may need to cook them in batches.
6. Air fry until crispy for 10 to 15 minutes, shaking the basket a couple of times for even cooking.
7. Serve immediately.

# Homemade Fish Sticks

**SERVES 4**

**PREP TIME:** 15 minutes
**COOK TIME:** 10 to 15 minutes

**2 eggs**
**4 fish fillets**
**66 g whole-wheat flour**
**1 tsp. seasoned salt**
**189 g whole-wheat panko bread crumbs**
**½ tbsp. dried parsley flakes**
**Cooking spray**

1. Preheat the air fryer to 200°C. Spray the air fryer basket lightly with cooking spray.
2. Cut the fish fillets lengthwise into "sticks."
3. In a shallow bowl, mix the whole-wheat flour and seasoned salt.
4. In a small bowl, whisk the eggs with 1 tsp. of water.
5. In another shallow bowl, mix the panko bread crumbs and parsley flakes.
6. Coat each fish stick in the seasoned flour, then in the egg mixture, and dredge them in the panko bread crumbs.
7. Place the fish sticks in the air fryer basket in a single layer and lightly spray the fish sticks with cooking spray. You may need to cook them in batches.
8. Air fry for 5 to 8 minutes. Flip the fish sticks over and lightly spray with the cooking spray. Air fry until golden brown and crispy, 5 to 7 more minutes.
9. Serve warm.

# Sesame Glazed Salmon

**SERVES 4**

**PREP TIME:** 5 minutes
**COOK TIME:** 12 to 16 minutes

**1 tbsp. brown sugar**
**1 tbsp. toasted sesame oil**
**1 tsp. minced garlic**
**¼ tsp. minced ginger**
**3 tbsps. soy sauce**
**1 tbsp. rice wine or dry sherry**
**4 (170-g) salmon fillets, skin-on**
**½ tbsp. sesame seeds**
**Cooking spray**

1. In a small bowl, mix the soy sauce, rice wine, brown sugar, toasted sesame oil, garlic, and ginger.
2. Place the salmon in a shallow baking dish and pour the marinade over the fillets. Cover and refrigerate for at least 1 hour, turning the fillets occasionally to coat in the marinade.
3. Preheat the air fryer to 190°C. Spray the air fryer basket lightly with cooking spray.
4. Shake off as much marinade as possible and place the fillets, skin-side down, in the air fryer basket in a single layer. Reserve the marinade. You may need to cook them in batches.
5. Air fry for 8 to 10 minutes. Brush the tops of the salmon fillets with the reserved marinade and sprinkle with sesame seeds.
6. Increase the temperature to 200°C and air fry for 2 to 5 more minutes for medium, 1 to 3 minutes for medium rare, or 4 to 6 minutes for well done.
7. Serve warm.

# Spicy Orange Prawn

PREP TIME: 20 minutes
COOK TIME: 10 to 15 minutes

¼ to ½ tsp. cayenne pepper
80 ml orange juice
3 tsps. minced garlic
1 tsp. Old Bay seasoning
454 g medium prawns, peeled and deveined, with tails off
Cooking spray

1. In a medium bowl, combine the orange juice, garlic, Old Bay seasoning, and cayenne pepper.
2. Dry the prawns with paper towels to remove excess water.
3. Add the prawns to the marinade and stir to evenly coat. Cover with clingfilm and place in the refrigerator for 30 minutes so the prawns can soak up the marinade.
4. Preheat the air fryer to 200ºC. Spray the air fryer basket lightly with cooking spray.
5. Place the prawns into the air fryer basket. Air fry for 5 minutes. Shake the basket and lightly spray with olive oil. Air fry until the prawns are opaque and crisp, 5 to 10 more minutes.
6. Serve immediately.

# Seasoned Breaded Prawn

PREP TIME: 15 minutes
COOK TIME: 10 to 15 minutes

2 large eggs
2 tsps. Old Bay seasoning, divided
½ tsp. garlic powder
½ tsp. onion powder
454 g large prawns, deveined, with tails on
62 g whole-wheat panko bread crumbs
Cooking spray

1. Preheat the air fryer to 190ºC.
2. Spray the air fryer basket lightly with cooking spray.
3. In a medium bowl, mix together 1 tsp. of Old Bay seasoning, garlic powder, and onion powder. Add the prawns and toss with the seasoning mix to lightly coat.
4. In a separate small bowl, whisk the eggs with 1 tsp. water.
5. In a shallow bowl, mix together the remaining 1 tsp. Old Bay seasoning and the panko bread crumbs.
6. Dip each prawns in the egg mixture and dredge in the bread crumb mixture to evenly coat.
7. Place the prawns in the air fryer basket, in a single layer. Lightly spray the prawns with cooking spray. You many need to cook the prawns in batches.
8. Air fry for 10 to 15 minutes, or until the prawns is cooked through and crispy, shaking the basket at 5-minute intervals to redistribute and evenly cook.
9. Serve immediately.

# Marinated Salmon Fillets

PREP TIME: 10 minutes
COOK TIME: 15 to 20 minutes

1 tbsp. olive oil
1 tsp. mustard powder
1 tsp. ground ginger
60 ml soy sauce
60 ml rice wine vinegar
1 tbsp. brown sugar
½ tsp. freshly ground black pepper
½ tsp. minced garlic
4 (170-g) salmon fillets, skin-on
Cooking spray

1. In a small bowl, combine the soy sauce, rice wine vinegar, brown sugar, olive oil, mustard powder, ginger, black pepper, and garlic to make a marinade.
2. Place the fillets in a shallow baking dish and pour the marinade over them. Cover the baking dish and marinate for at least 1 hour in the refrigerator, turning the fillets occasionally to keep them coated in the marinade.
3. Preheat the air fryer to 190°C. Spray the air fryer basket lightly with cooking spray.
4. Shake off as much marinade as possible from the fillets and place them, skin-side down, in the air fryer basket in a single layer. You may need to cook the fillets in batches.
5. Air fry for 15 to 20 minutes for well done. The minimum internal temperature should be 65°C at the thickest part of the fillets.
6. Serve hot.

# Vegetable with Fish Tacos

PREP TIME: 10 minutes
COOK TIME: 9 to 12 minutes

125 g low-sodium salsa
90 g low-fat Greek yoghurt
454 g white fish fillets
2 tsps. olive oil
3 tbsps. freshly squeezed lemon juice, divided
30 g chopped red cabbage
1 large carrot, grated
4 soft low-sodium whole-wheat tortillas

1. Preheat the air fryer to 200°C.
2. Brush the fish with the olive oil and sprinkle with 1 tbsp. of lemon juice. Air fry in the air fryer basket for 9 to 12 minutes, or until the fish just flakes when tested with a fork.
3. Meanwhile, in a medium bowl, stir together the remaining 2 tbsps. of lemon juice, the red cabbage, carrot, salsa, and yoghurt.
4. When the fish is cooked, remove it from the air fryer basket and break it up into large pieces.
5. Offer the fish, tortillas, and the cabbage mixture, and let each person assemble a taco.
6. Serve immediately.

# Cajun-Style Fish Tacos

**SERVES 6**

| | | |
|---|---|---|
| PREP TIME: 5 minutes<br>COOK TIME: 10 to 15 minutes | 1 (397-g) package coleslaw mix<br>12 corn tortillas<br>2 tsps. avocado oil | 1 tbsp. Cajun seasoning<br>4 tilapia fillets<br>2 limes, cut into wedges |

1. Preheat the air fryer to 190°C. Line the air fryer basket with parchment paper.
2. In a medium, shallow bowl, mix the avocado oil and the Cajun seasoning to make a marinade. Add the tilapia fillets and coat evenly.
3. Place the fillets in the basket in a single layer, leaving room between each fillet. You may need to cook in batches.
4. Air fry until the fish is cooked and easily flakes with a fork, 10 to 15 minutes.
5. Assemble the tacos by placing some of the coleslaw mix in each tortilla. Add ⅓ of a tilapia fillet to each tortilla. Squeeze some lime juice over the top of each taco and serve.

# Crispy Tuna Sliders

**SERVES 4**

| | |
|---|---|
| PREP TIME: 15 minutes<br>COOK TIME: 10 to 15 minutes | 1 tbsp. sriracha<br>¾ tsp. black pepper<br>3 (142-g) tins tuna, packed in water<br>85 g whole-wheat panko bread crumbs<br>30 g shredded Parmesan cheese<br>10 whole-wheat slider buns<br>Cooking spray |

1. Preheat the air fryer to 180°C.
2. Spray the air fryer basket lightly with cooking spray.
3. In a medium bowl combine the tuna, bread crumbs, Parmesan cheese, sriracha, and black pepper and stir to combine.
4. Form the mixture into 10 patties.
5. Place the patties in the air fryer basket in a single layer. Spray the patties lightly with cooking spray. You may need to cook them in batches.
6. Air fry for 6 to 8 minutes. Turn the patties over and lightly spray with cooking spray. Air fry until golden brown and crisp, another 4 to 7 more minutes. Serve warm.

# Country Prawn

**SERVES 4**

| | |
|---|---|
| PREP TIME: 10 minutes<br>COOK TIME: 15 to 20 minutes | 1 courgette, cut into bite-sized pieces<br>1 red pepper, cut into chunks<br>1 tbsp. Old Bay seasoning<br>2 tbsps. olive oil<br>454 g large prawns, deveined, with tails on<br>454 g smoked turkey sausage, cut into thick slices<br>2 corn cobs, quartered<br>Cooking spray |

1. Preheat the air fryer to 200°C. Spray the air fryer basket lightly with cooking spray.
2. In a large bowl, mix the prawns, turkey sausage, corn, courgette, pepper, and Old Bay seasoning, and toss to coat with the spices. Add the olive oil and toss again until evenly coated.
3. Spread the mixture in the air fryer basket in a single layer. You will need to cook in batches.
4. Air fry for 15 to 20 minutes, or until cooked through, shaking the basket every 5 minutes for even cooking.
5. Serve immediately.

# Crispy Cod Cakes and Salad Greens

**SERVES 4**

| | |
|---|---|
| **PREP TIME:** 15 minutes<br>**COOK TIME:** 12 minutes | ¼ tsp. salt<br>¼ tsp. pepper<br>½ tsp. smoked paprika<br>1 large egg, beaten<br>454 g cod fillets, cut into chunks<br>30 g packed fresh basil leaves<br>3 cloves garlic, crushed<br>125 g panko bread crumbs<br>Cooking spray<br>Salad greens, for serving |

1. In a food processor, pulse cod, basil, garlic, smoked paprika, salt, and pepper until cod is finely chopped, stirring occasionally. Form into 8 patties, about 4-cm in diameter. Dip each first into the egg, then into the panko, patting to adhere. Spray with oil on one side.
2. Preheat the air fryer to 200ºC.
3. Working in batches, place half the cakes in the basket, oil-side down; spray with oil. Air fry for 12 minutes, until golden brown and cooked through.
4. Serve cod cakes with salad greens.

# Cajun Salmon Burgers

**SERVES 4**

| | |
|---|---|
| **PREP TIME:** 10 minutes<br>**COOK TIME:** 10 to 15 minutes | 4 tbsps. light mayonnaise<br>2 tsps. Cajun seasoning<br>2 tsps. dry mustard<br>4 whole-wheat buns<br>4 (142-g) tins pink salmon in water, any skin and bones removed, drained<br>2 eggs, beaten<br>125 g whole-wheat bread crumbs<br>Cooking spray |

1. In a medium bowl, mix the salmon, egg, bread crumbs, mayonnaise, Cajun seasoning, and dry mustard. Cover with clingfilm and refrigerate for 30 minutes.
2. Preheat the air fryer to 180ºC. Spray the air fryer basket lightly with cooking spray.
3. Shape the mixture into four 1-cm-thick patties about the same size as the buns.
4. Place the salmon patties in the air fryer basket in a single layer and lightly spray the tops with cooking spray. You may need to cook them in batches.
5. Air fry for 6 to 8 minutes. Turn the patties over and lightly spray with cooking spray. Air fry until crispy on the outside, 4 to 7 more minutes.
6. Serve on whole-wheat buns.

# Green Curry Prawn

**SERVES 4**

| | |
|---|---|
| PREP TIME: 15 minutes<br>COOK TIME: 5 minutes | **454 g jumbo raw prawns, peeled and deveined**<br>**15 g chopped fresh Thai basil or sweet basil**<br>**15 g chopped fresh coriander**<br>**1 to 2 tbsps. Thai green curry paste**<br>**2 tbsps. coconut oil, melted**<br>**1 tbsp. half-and-half or coconut milk**<br>**1 tsp. fish sauce**<br>**1 tsp. soy sauce**<br>**1 tsp. minced fresh ginger**<br>**1 clove garlic, minced** |

1. In a baking pan, combine the curry paste, coconut oil, half-and-half, fish sauce, soy sauce, ginger, and garlic. Whisk until well combined.
2. Add the prawns and toss until well coated. Marinate at room temperature for 15 to 30 minutes.
3. Preheat the air fryer to 200°C.
4. Place the pan in the air fryer basket. Air fry for 5 minutes, stirring halfway through the cooking time.
5. Transfer the prawns to a serving bowl or platter. Garnish with the basil and coriander. Serve immediately.

# Air Fried Spring Rolls

**SERVES 4**

| | |
|---|---|
| PREP TIME: 10 minutes<br>COOK TIME: 17 to 22 minutes | **2 113-g) tins tiny prawns, drained**<br>**4 tsps. soy sauce**<br>**2 tsps. minced garlic**<br>**40 g finely sliced cabbage**<br>**135 g matchstick cut carrots**<br>**Salt and freshly ground black pepper, to taste**<br>**16 square spring roll wrappers**<br>**Cooking spray** |

1. Preheat the air fryer to 190°C.
2. Spray the air fryer basket lightly with cooking spray. Spray a medium sauté pan with cooking spray.
3. Add the garlic to the sauté pan and cook over medium heat until fragrant, 30 to 45 seconds. Add the cabbage and carrots and sauté until the vegetables are slightly tender, about 5 minutes.
4. Add the prawns and soy sauce and season with salt and pepper, then stir to combine. Sauté until the moisture has evaporated, 2 more minutes. Set aside to cool.
5. Place a spring roll wrapper on a work surface so it looks like a diamond. Place 1 tbsp. of the prawn mixture on the lower end of the wrapper.
6. Roll the wrapper away from you halfway, then fold in the right and left sides, like an envelope. Continue to roll to the very end, using a little water to seal the edge. Repeat with the remaining wrappers and filling.
7. Place the spring rolls in the air fryer basket in a single layer, leaving room between each roll. Lightly spray with cooking spray. You may need to cook them in batches.
8. Air fry for 5 minutes. Turn the rolls over, lightly spray with cooking spray, and air fry until heated through and the rolls start to brown, 5 to 10 more minutes. Cool for 5 minutes before serving.

# CHAPTER 5
# POULTRY

# Easy Turkey Drumsticks

## SERVES 2

PREP TIME: 25 minutes
COOK TIME: 23 minutes

2 turkey drumsticks
60 ml coconut milk
1 tbsp. red curry paste
½ tsp. cayenne pepper
1½ tbsps. minced ginger
1 tsp. salt, or more to taste
⅓ tsp. ground pepper, to more to taste

1. First of all, place turkey drumsticks with all ingredients in your refrigerator, let it marinate overnight.
2. Cook turkey drumsticks at 190°C for 23 minutes, make sure to flip them over at half-time. Serve with the salad on the side.

# Turkey and Gravy

## SERVES 6

PREP TIME: 50 minutes
COOK TIME: 20 minutes

2 tbsps. turkey stock
2 tbsps. whole-grain mustard
1 tbsp. butter
2 tsps. butter, softened
1 tsp. dried sage
2 sprigs rosemary, chopped
1 tsp. salt
¼ tsp. freshly ground black pepper, or more to taste
1 whole turkey breast

1. Start by preheating your Air Fryer to 180°C.
2. To make the rub, combine 2 tbsps. of butter, sage, rosemary, salt, and pepper, mix well to combine and spread it evenly over the surface of the turkey breast.
3. Roast for 20 minutes in an Air Fryer cooking basket. Flip the turkey breast over and roast for a further 15 to 16 minutes. Now, flip it back over and roast for 12 minutes or more.
4. While the turkey is roasting, whisk the other ingredients in a saucepan. After that, spread the gravy all over the turkey breast.
5. Let the turkey rest for a few minutes before carving. Bon appétit!

# Herbed Turkey Breasts with Mustard

SERVES 4

PREP TIME: 1 hour
COOK TIME: 53 minutes

**1½ tbsps. olive oil**
**1½ tbsps. hot mustard**
**1 tsp. smoked cayenne pepper**
**1 tsp. fine sea salt**
**½ tsp. dried thyme**
**680g turkey breasts**
**½ tsp. dried sage**
**3 whole star anise**

1. Set your Air Fryer to cook at 185°C.
2. Brush the turkey breast with olive oil and sprinkle with seasonings.
3. Cook at 185°C for 45 minutes, turning twice. Now, pause the machine and spread the cooked breast with the hot mustard.
4. Air-fry for 6 to 8 more minutes. Let it rest before slicing and serving. Bon appétit!

# Roasted Chicken Leg

SERVES 6

PREP TIME: 20 minutes
COOK TIME: 18 minutes

**½ tsp. smoked cayenne pepper**
**2 tbsps. olive oil**
**2 large-sized tomatoes, chopped**
**3 cloves garlic, minced**
**½ tsp. dried oregano**
**6 chicken legs**
**A freshly ground nutmeg**

1. In a mixing dish, thoroughly combine all ingredients. Place in the refrigerator and let it marinate overnight.
2. Lay the vegetables onto the bottom of an Air Fryer cooking basket. Top with the chicken legs.
3. Roast chicken legs at 190°C for 18 minutes, turning halfway through. Serve with hoisin sauce.

# Chicken Breast with Coriander and Lime

PREP TIME: 10 minutes
COOK TIME: 15 minutes

**For the Chicken:**
1 tsp. smoked paprika
1 tsp. ground fennel seeds
1 tsp. turmeric
1 diced large onion
1 tbsp. avocado oil
1 tsp. garam masala
455-g chicken breast, boneless & skinless
2 tsps. minced ginger
2 tsps. minced garlic cloves
nonstick cooking oil spray
salt & cayenne pepper, to taste
**To Top:**
15 g chopped coriander
2 tsps. juiced lime

1. Make slight piercing all over the chicken breast then set aside.
2. Using a large mixing bowl add in all the remaining ingredients and combine together.
3. Add the pierced chicken breast into the bowl then set aside for an hour to marinate.
4. Transfer the marinated chicken and veggies into the fryer basket then coat with the cooking oil spray.
5. Roast for 15 minutes at 180ºC then serve and enjoy with a garnish of coriander topped with the juiced lime.

# Chicken with Lettuce

PREP TIME: 15 minutes
COOK TIME: 14 minutes

455 g chicken breast tenders, chopped into bite-size pieces
1 tbsp. olive oil
1 tbsp. fajita seasoning
½ onion, thinly sliced
½ red pepper, seeded and thinly sliced
½ green pepper, seeded and thinly sliced
1 tsp. salt
Juice of ½ lime
8 large lettuce leaves
90 g prepared guacamole

1. Preheat the air fryer to 205°C.
2. In a large bowl, combine the chicken, onion, and peppers. Drizzle with the olive oil and toss until thoroughly coated. Add the fajita seasoning and salt and toss again.
3. Working in batches if necessary, arrange the chicken and vegetables in a single layer in the air fryer basket. Pausing halfway through the cooking time to shake the basket, air fry for 14 minutes, or until the vegetables are tender and a thermometer inserted into the thickest piece of chicken registers 75ºC.
4. Transfer the mixture to a serving platter and drizzle with the fresh lime juice. Serve with the lettuce leaves and top with the guacamole.

# Rosemary Turkey Roast

## SERVES 6

PREP TIME: 50 minutes
COOK TIME: 45 minutes

1.1kg turkey breasts
1 onion, chopped
1 celery stick, chopped
1 tbsp. fresh rosemary, chopped
1 tsp. sea salt
½ tsp. ground black pepper

1. Start by preheating your Air Fryer to 180°C. Spritz the sides and bottom of the cooking basket with a nonstick cooking spray.
2. Place the turkey in the cooking basket. Add the rosemary, salt, and black pepper. Roast for 30 minutes in the preheated Air Fryer.
3. Add the onion and celery and roast for an additional 15 minutes. Bon appétit!

# Turkey and Mustard Sauce

## SERVES 4

PREP TIME: 13 minutes
COOK TIME: 18 minutes

½ tsp. hot paprika
2 tbsps. melted butter
1 tsp. fine sea salt
½ tsp. cumin powder
910 g turkey breasts, quartered
2 cloves garlic, smashed
Freshly cracked mixed peppercorns, to taste
Fresh juice of 1 lemon
For the Mustard Sauce:
1½ tbsps. mayonnaise
370 g Greek yoghurt
½ tbsp. yellow mustard

1. Grab a medium-sized mixing dish and combine together the garlic and melted butter, rub this mixture evenly over the surface of the turkey.
2. Add the cumin powder, followed by paprika, salt, peppercorns, and lemon juice. Place in your refrigerator for at least 55 minutes.
3. Set your Air Fryer to cook at 190°C. Roast the turkey for 18 minutes, turning halfway through, roast in batches.
4. In the meantime, make the mustard sauce by mixing all ingredients for the sauce. Serve warm roasted turkey with the mustard sauce. Bon appétit!

# White Wine Chicken Breast

| PREP TIME: 30 minutes<br>COOK TIME: 28 minutes | 3 medium-sized boneless chicken breasts, cut into small pieces<br>1½ tbsps. sesame oil<br>½ tsp. grated fresh ginger<br>80 ml coconut milk<br>½ tsp. sea salt flakes<br>3 green garlic stalks, finely chopped<br>120 ml dry white wine<br>½ tsp. fresh thyme leaves, minced<br>⅓ tsp. freshly cracked black pepper |
|---|---|

1. Warm the sesame oil in a deep sauté pan over a moderate heat. Then, sauté the green garlic until just fragrant.
2. Remove the pan from the heat and pour in the coconut milk and the white wine. After that, add the thyme, sea salt, fresh ginger, and freshly cracked black pepper. Scrape this mixture into a baking dish.
3. Stir in the chicken chunks.
4. Cook in the preheated Air Fryer for 28 minutes at 170ºC. Serve on individual plates and eat warm.

# Turkey Sausage and Cauliflower

| PREP TIME: 45 minutes<br>COOK TIME: 28 minutes | ⅓ tsp. dried oregano<br>½ tsp. salt<br>455 g turkey mince<br>1 tsp. garlic pepper<br>1 tsp. garlic powder | 25 g onions, chopped<br>½ head cauliflower, broken into florets<br>⅓ tsp. dried basil<br>½ tsp. dried thyme, chopped |
|---|---|---|

1. In a mixing bowl, thoroughly combine the turkey mince, garlic pepper, garlic powder, oregano, salt, and onion, stir well to combine. Spritz a nonstick frying pan with pan spray, form the mixture into 4 sausages.
2. Then, cook the sausage over medium heat until they are no longer pink, for approximately 12 minutes.
3. Arrange the cauliflower florets at the bottom of a baking dish. Sprinkle with thyme and basil, spritz with pan spray. Top with the turkey sausages.
4. Roast for 28 minutes at 190ºC, turning once halfway through. Eat warm.

# Turkey and Tabasco Sauce

| PREP TIME: 15 minutes<br>COOK TIME: 22 minutes | 680g turkey mince<br>6 whole eggs, well beaten<br>3 cloves garlic, finely minced<br>1 tsp. ground black pepper<br>½ tsp. sea salt | ⅓ tsp. smoked paprika<br>2 egg whites, beaten<br>Tabasco sauce, for drizzling<br>2 tbsps. sesame oil<br>2 leeks, chopped |
|---|---|---|

1. Warm the oil in a pan over moderate heat, then, sweat the leeks and garlic until tender, stir periodically.
2. Next, grease 6 oven safe ramekins with pan spray. Divide the sautéed mixture among six ramekins.
3. In a bowl, beat the eggs and egg whites using a wire whisk. Stir in the smoked paprika, salt and black pepper, whisk until everything is thoroughly combined. Divide the egg mixture among the ramekins.
4. Air-fry approximately 22 minutes at 175ºC. Drizzle Tabasco sauce over each portion and serve.

# Mayo-Dijon Chicken

PREP TIME: 5 minutes
COOK TIME: 13 to 16 minutes

1 tbsp. coconut aminos
1 tsp. Italian seasoning
1 tsp. sea salt
1 tbsp. Dijon mustard
110 g mayonnaise
1 tbsp. freshly squeezed lemon juice (optional)
½ tsp. freshly ground black pepper
¼ tsp. cayenne pepper
680g boneless, skinless chicken breasts or thighs

1. In a small bowl, combine the mayonnaise, mustard, lemon juice (if using), coconut aminos, Italian seasoning, salt, black pepper, and cayenne pepper.
2. Place the chicken in a shallow dish or large zip-top plastic bag. Add the marinade, making sure all the pieces are coated. Cover and refrigerate for at least 30 minutes or up to 4 hours.
3. Set the air fryer to 205°C. Arrange the chicken in a single layer in the air fryer basket, working in batches if necessary. Roast for 7 minutes. Flip the chicken and continue cooking for 6 to 9 minutes or more, until an instant-read thermometer reads 70°C.

# Spicy Chicken Roll-Up and Monterey Jack

PREP TIME: 10 minutes
COOK TIME: 14 to 17 minutes

910 g boneless, skinless chicken breasts or thighs
1 tsp. chilli powder
115 g canned diced green chillies
Avocado oil spray
½ tsp. smoked paprika
½ tsp. ground cumin
Sea salt
Freshly ground black pepper
170 g Monterey Jack cheese, shredded

1. Place the chicken in a large zip-top bag or between two pieces of clingfilm. Using a meat mallet or heavy frying pan, pound the chicken until it is about ½ cm thick.
2. In a small bowl, combine the chilli powder, smoked paprika, cumin, and salt and pepper to taste. Sprinkle both sides of the chicken with the seasonings.
3. Sprinkle the chicken with the Monterey Jack cheese, then the diced green chiles.
4. Roll up each piece of chicken from the long side, tucking in the ends as you go. Secure the roll-up with a toothpick.
5. Set the air fryer to 180°C. Spray the outside of the chicken with avocado oil. Place the chicken in a single layer in the basket, working in batches if necessary, and roast for 7 minutes. Flip and roast for another 7 to 10 minutes, until an instant-read thermometer reads 70°C.
6. Remove the chicken from the air fryer and allow it to rest for about 5 minutes before serving.

# CHAPTER 6
# BEEF

# Super Simple Steaks

**PREP TIME:** 5 minutes
**COOK TIME:** 14 minutes

**230 g quality cuts steak**
**What you'll need from the store cupboard:**
**Salt and black pepper, to taste**

1. Preheat the Air fryer to 200°C and grease an Air fryer basket.
2. Season the steaks evenly with salt and black pepper and transfer into the Air fryer basket.
3. Roast for about 14 minutes and dish out to serve.

# Smoky Beef Burgers

**PREP TIME:** 20 minutes
**COOK TIME:** 10 minutes

**450 g ground beef**
**4 whole-wheat hamburger buns, split and toasted**
**What you'll need from the store cupboard:**
**½ tsp. garlic powder**
**½ tsp. onion powder**
**15 ml Worcestershire sauce**
**1 tsp. Maggi seasoning sauce**
**3-4 drops liquid smoke**
**1 tsp. dried parsley**
**Salt and ground black pepper, as required**

1. Preheat the Air fryer to 175°C and grease an Air fryer basket.
2. Mix the beef, sauces, liquid smoke, parsley, and spices in a bowl.
3. Make 4 equal-sized patties from the beef mixture and arrange in the Air fryer basket.
4. Roast for about 10 minutes and dish out to serve on a bun.

# Delicious Beef Jerky

**SERVES 3**

PREP TIME: 20 minutes
COOK TIME: 1 hour

**450 g beef silverside, cut into thin strips**
**What you'll need from the store cupboard:**
**1 tsp. cayenne pepper**
**½ tsp. smoked paprika**
**½ tsp. ground black pepper**
**100 g dark brown sugar**
**115 ml soy sauce**
**60 ml Worcestershire sauce**
**15 ml chilli pepper sauce**
**15 ml hickory liquid smoke**
**1 tsp. garlic powder**
**1 tsp. onion powder**

1. Preheat the Air fryer to 180°C and grease an Air fryer basket.
2. Mix the brown sugar, all sauces, liquid smoke, and spices in a bowl.
3. Coat the beef strips with this marinade generously and marinate overnight.
4. Place half of the beef strips in the Air fryer basket in a single layer.
5. Arrange a cooking rack over the strips and layer with the remaining beef strips.
6. Roast for about 1 hour and dish out to serve.

# Beef Stuffed Peppers

**SERVES 4**

PREP TIME: 20 minutes
COOK TIME: 26 minutes

**4 peppers, tops and seeds removed**
**½ medium onion, chopped**
**450 g lean ground beef**
**100 g jasmine rice, cooked**
**75 g light cheddar cheese, shredded and divided**
**What you'll need from the store cupboard:**
**½ tsp. red chilli powder**
**1 tsp. olive oil**
**2 garlic cloves, minced**
**1 tsp. dried basil, crushed**
**1 tsp. garlic salt**
**Ground black pepper, as required**
**225 g tomato passata, divided**
**2 tsps. Worcestershire sauce**

1. Preheat the Air fryer to 200°C and grease an Air fryer basket.
2. Heat olive oil in a medium frying pan over medium heat and add onion and garlic.
3. Sauté for about 5 minutes and add the ground beef, basil, and spices.
4. Bake for about 10 minutes and drain off the excess grease from frying pan.
5. Stir in the rice, half of the cheese, 2/3 of the tomato passata and Worcestershire sauce and mix well.
6. Stuff the beef mixture in each pepper and arrange the peppers in the Air fryer basket.
7. Bake for about 7 minutes and top with the remaining tomato sauce and cheese.
8. Bake for 4 more minutes and dish out in a bowl to serve warm.

# Honey Mustard Meatballs

SERVES 8

PREP TIME: 15 minutes
COOK TIME: 15 minutes

**15 g cheddar cheese, grated**
**2 onions, chopped**
**450 g ground beef**
**4 tbsps. fresh basil, chopped**
**What you'll need from the store cupboard:**
**15 g honey**
**2 tsps. garlic paste**
**Salt and black pepper, to taste**
**2 tsps. mustard**

1. Preheat the Air fryer to 385°C and grease an Air fryer basket.
2. Mix all the ingredients in a bowl until well combined.
3. Shape the mixture into equal-sized balls gently and arrange the meatballs in the Air fryer basket.
4. Air fry for about 15 minutes and dish out to serve warm.

# Flank Steak Beef

SERVES 4

PREP TIME: 10 minutes
COOK TIME: 20 minutes

**450 g flank steaks, sliced**
**28 g xanthan gum**
**What you'll need from the store cupboard:**
**1 tbsp. garlic, minced**
**115 ml water**
**150 g sugar**
**10 ml rapeseed oil**
**½ tsp. ginger**
**115 ml soy sauce**

1. Preheat the Air fryer to 200°C and grease an Air fryer basket.
2. Coat the steaks with xanthan gum on both the sides and transfer into the Air fryer basket.
3. Roast for about 10 minutes and dish out in a platter.
4. Meanwhile, cook rest of the ingredients for the sauce in a saucepan.
5. Bring to a boil and pour over the steak slices to serve.

# Cheesy Beef Meatballs

**SERVES 8**

PREP TIME: 20 minutes
COOK TIME: 34 minutes

**2 large eggs**
**900 g ground beef**
**150 g panko breadcrumbs**
**30 g Parmigiana-Reggiano cheese, grated**
**15 g fresh parsley, chopped**
**What you'll need from the store cupboard:**
**Salt and black pepper, to taste**
**1 small garlic clove, chopped**
**1 tsp. dried oregano, crushed**

1. Preheat the Air fryer to 175°C and grease an Air fryer basket.
2. Mix all the ingredients in a bowl until well combined.
3. Shape the mixture 5-centimetre balls gently and arrange half of the meatballs in the Air fryer basket.
4. Flip the side and roast for about 12 minutes.
5. Roast for about 5 minutes more and dish out to serve warm.

# Simple Beef Burgers

**SERVES 6**

PREP TIME: 20 minutes
COOK TIME: 12 minutes

**12 dinner rolls**
**900 g ground beef**
**12 cheddar cheese slices**
**What you'll need from the store cupboard:**
**90 ml tomato ketchup**
**Salt and black pepper, to taste**

1. Preheat the Air fryer to 200°C and grease an Air fryer basket.
2. Mix the beef, salt and black pepper in a bowl.
3. Make small equal-sized patties from the beef mixture and arrange half of patties in the Air fryer basket.
4. Grill for about 12 minutes and top each patty with 1 cheese slice.
5. Arrange the patties between rolls and drizzle with ketchup.
6. Repeat with the remaining batch and dish out to serve hot.

# Beef and Mushroom Meatloaf

**SERVES 4**

| | |
|---|---|
| PREP TIME: 15 minutes<br>COOK TIME: 25 minutes | 1 egg, lightly beaten<br>2 mushrooms, thickly sliced<br>450 g lean ground beef<br>1 small onion, finely chopped<br>25 g dry breadcrumbs<br>**What you'll need from the store cupboard:**<br>Salt and ground black pepper, as required<br>15 ml olive oil |

1. Preheat the Air fryer to 200°C and grease an Air fryer basket.
2. Mix the beef, onion, olive oil, breadcrumbs, egg, salt, and black pepper in a bowl until well combined.
3. Shape the mixture into loaves and top with mushroom slices.
4. Arrange the loaves in the Air fryer basket and roast for about 25 minutes.
5. Cut into desired size wedges and serve warm.

# Classic Skirt Steak Strips with Veggies

**SERVES 4**

| | |
|---|---|
| PREP TIME: 10 minutes<br>COOK TIME: 17 minutes | 1 onion, cut into half rings<br>1 (340 gram) skirt steak, cut into thin strips<br>230 g fresh mushrooms, quartered<br>170 g mangetout<br>**What you'll need from the store cupboard:**<br>60 ml olive oil, divided<br>30 ml sauce<br>40 g honey<br>Salt and black pepper, to taste |

1. Preheat the Air fryer to 200°C and grease an Air fryer basket.
2. Mix 30 ml of oil, soy sauce and honey in a bowl and coat steak strips with this marinade.
3. Put vegetables, remaining oil, salt and black pepper in another bowl and toss well.
4. Transfer the steak strips and vegetables in the Air fryer basket and roast for about 17 minutes.
5. Dish out and serve warm.

# Beef Cheeseburgers

**SERVES 2**

| | |
|---|---|
| PREP TIME: 15 minutes<br>COOK TIME: 12 minutes | 2 salad leaves<br>2 dinner rolls, cut into half<br>230 g ground beef<br>2 tbsps. fresh coriander, minced<br>2 slices cheddar cheese<br>**What you'll need from the store cupboard:**<br>1 garlic clove, minced<br>Salt and black pepper, to taste |

1. Preheat the Air fryer to 200°C and grease an Air fryer basket.
2. Mix the beef, garlic, coriander, salt, and black pepper in a bowl.
3. Make 2 equal-sized patties from the beef mixture and arrange in the Air fryer basket.
4. Grill for about 11 minutes and top each patty with 1 cheese slice.
5. Grill for about 1 more minute and dish out in a platter.
6. Place dinner rolls in a serving platter and arrange salad leaf between each dinner roll.
7. Top with 1 patty and immediately serve.

# Beef and Veggie Kebabs

**SERVES 4**

| PREP TIME: 20 minutes<br>COOK TIME: 12 minutes | 450 g sirloin steak, cut into chunks<br>225 g baby Bella mushrooms, stems removed<br>1 large pepper, seeded and cut into 2.5-centimetre pieces<br>1 red onion, cut into 2.5-centimetre pieces<br>**What you'll need from the store cupboard:**<br>1 tsp. brown sugar<br>½ tsp. ground cumin<br>60 ml soy sauce<br>60 ml olive oil<br>1 tbsp. garlic, minced<br>Salt and black pepper, to taste |
|---|---|

1. Preheat the Air fryer to 200°C and grease an Air fryer basket.
2. Mix soy sauce, oil, garlic, brown sugar, cumin, salt, and black pepper in a large bowl.
3. Coat the steak cubes generously with marinade and refrigerate to marinate for about 30 minutes.
4. Thread the steak cubes, mushrooms, pepper, and onion onto metal skewers.
5. Place the skewers in the Air fryer basket and roast for about 12 minutes, flipping once in between.
6. Dish out in a platter and serve hot.


# Beef with Veggie Spring Rolls

**SERVES 8**

| PREP TIME: 10 minutes<br>COOK TIME: 35 minutes | 55 g Asian rice noodles, soaked in warm water, drained and cut into small lengths<br>1 packet spring roll skins<br>200 g ground beef<br>1 small onion, chopped<br>70 g fresh mixed vegetables<br>**What you'll need from the store cupboard:**<br>60 ml olive oil<br>Salt and black pepper, to taste |
|---|---|

1. Preheat the Air fryer to 175°C and grease an Air fryer basket.
2. Heat olive oil in a pan and add the onion and garlic.
3. Sauté for about 5 minutes and stir in the beef.
4. Roast for about 5 minutes and add vegetables and soy sauce.
5. Roast for about 7 minutes and stir in the noodles.
6. Place the spring rolls skin onto a smooth surface and put the filling mixture diagonally in it.
7. Fold in both sides to seal properly and brush with oil.
8. Arrange the rolls in batches in the Air fryer basket and roast for about 13 minutes, tossing in between.
9. Roast for about 15 minutes, flipping once in between and dish out in a platter.

# CHAPTER 7
# PORK

# Caramelized Pork

**SERVES 6**

PREP TIME: 10 minutes
COOK TIME: 17 minutes

**900 g pork shoulder, cut into 4-centimetre thick cubes**
**What you'll need from the store cupboard:**
**80 ml soy sauce**
**25 g sugar**
**20 g honey**

1. Preheat the Air fryer to 170°C and grease an Air fryer basket.
2. Mix all the ingredients in a large bowl and coat chops well.
3. Cover and refrigerate for about 8 hours.
4. Arrange the chops in the Air fryer basket and roast for about 10 minutes, flipping once in between.
5. Set the Air fryer to 200°C and roast for 7 more minutes.
6. Dish out in a platter and serve hot.

# Sweet with Sour Pork Chops

**SERVES 4**

PREP TIME: 10 minutes
COOK TIME: 16 minutes

**6 pork loin chops**
**What you'll need from the store cupboard:**
**40 g honey**
**30 ml soy sauce**
**Salt and black pepper, to taste**
**2 garlic cloves, minced**
**15 ml balsamic vinegar**
**¼ tsp. ground ginger**

1. Preheat the Air fryer to 180°C and grease a baking tray.
2. Season the chops with a little salt and black pepper.
3. Mix rest of the ingredients in a large bowl and add chops.
4. Coat with marinade generously and cover to refrigerate for about 8 hours.
5. Arrange the chops in a baking tray and transfer into the Air fryer.
6. Air fry for about 16 minutes, flipping once in between and dish out to serve hot.

# Pork Spare Ribs

**PREP TIME:** 15 minutes
**COOK TIME:** 20 minutes

12 (2½-centimetre) pork spare ribs
60 g cornflour
**What you'll need from the store cupboard:**
30 ml soy sauce
60 ml olive oil
5-6 garlic cloves, minced
115 ml rice vinegar
Salt and black pepper, to taste

1. Preheat the Air fryer to 200°C and grease an Air fryer basket.
2. Mix the garlic, vinegar, soy sauce, salt, and black pepper in a large bowl.
3. Coat the ribs generously with this mixture and refrigerate to marinate overnight.
4. Place the cornflour in a shallow bowl and dredge the ribs in it.
5. Drizzle with olive oil and arrange the ribs in the Air fryer basket.
6. Roast for about 20 minutes, flipping once in between.
7. Dish out and serve hot.

# Smoky Flavoured Pork Ribs

**PREP TIME:** 10 minutes
**COOK TIME:** 13 minutes

350 g pork ribs
**What you'll need from the store cupboard:**
15 ml Worcestershire sauce
15 ml soy sauce
½ tsp. garlic powder
80 g honey, divided
175 ml BBQ sauce
30 ml tomato ketchup
Freshly ground white pepper, to taste

1. Preheat the Air fryer to 180°C and grease an Air fryer basket.
2. Mix 3 tbsps. of honey and remaining ingredients in a large bowl except the ribs.
3. Coat the pork ribs with marinade generously and cover to refrigerate for about 30 minutes.
4. Transfer the ribs into the Air fryer basket and roast for about 13 minutes.
5. Coat with remaining honey and serve hot.

# Red Wine Rib

**PREP TIME:** 20 minutes
**COOK TIME:** 10 minutes

**680 g short ribs**
**240 ml red wine**
**1 lemon, juiced**
**1 tsp. fresh ginger, grated**
**1 tsp. salt**
**1 tsp. black pepper**
**1 tsp. paprika**
**1 tsp. chipotle chilli powder**
**260 g keto tomato paste**
**1 tsp. garlic powder**
**1 tsp. cumin**

1. In a ceramic bowl, place the beef ribs, wine, lemon juice, ginger, salt, black pepper, paprika, and chipotle chilli powder. Cover and let it marinate for 3 hours in the refrigerator.
2. Discard the marinade and add the short ribs to the Air Fryer basket. Cook in the preheated Air fry at 190ºC for 10 minutes, turning them over halfway through the cooking time.
3. In the meantime, heat the saucepan over medium heat, add the reserved marinade and stir in the tomato paste, garlic powder, and cumin. Cook until the sauce has thickened slightly.
4. Pour the sauce over the warm ribs and serve immediately. Bon appétit!

# Breaded Pork Chops

**PREP TIME:** 15 minutes
**COOK TIME:** 15 minutes

**115 g Panko breadcrumbs**
**2 (170 gram) pork chops**
**35 g plain flour**
**1 egg**
**What you'll need from the store cupboard:**
**Salt and black pepper, to taste**
**15 ml rapeseed oil**

1. Preheat the Air fryer to 200°C and grease an Air fryer basket.
2. Season the chops with salt and black pepper.
3. Place the flour in a shallow bowl and whisk an egg in a second bowl.
4. Mix the breadcrumbs and rapeseed oil in a third bowl.
5. Coat the pork chops with flour, dip into egg and dredge into the breadcrumb mixture.
6. Arrange the chops in the Air fryer basket and grill for about 15 minutes, flipping once in between.
7. Dish out and serve hot.

# Pork Chops and Vermouth

## SERVES 6

PREP TIME: 22 minutes
COOK TIME: 18 minutes

2 tbsps. whole grain mustard
1 tsp. fine salt
2 tbsps. vermouth
4 centre-cut pork chops
½ tbsp. fresh basil, minced
⅓ tsp. freshly ground black pepper, or more to taste

1. Toss pork chops with other ingredients until they are well coated on both sides.
2. Air-fry your chops for 18 minutes at 210°C, turning once or twice.
3. Mound your favorite salad on a serving plate, top with pork chops and enjoy.

# Filling Pork Chops

## SERVES 2

PREP TIME: 20 minutes
COOK TIME: 12 minutes

2 (2.5-centimetre thick) pork chops
½ tbsp. fresh coriander, chopped
½ tbsp. fresh rosemary, chopped
½ tbsp. fresh parsley, chopped
What you'll need from the store cupboard:
1 tbsp. ground coriander
1 tsp. sugar
Salt, to taste
2 garlic cloves, minced
60 ml olive oil
15 g Dijon mustard

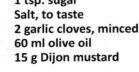

1. Preheat the Air fryer to 200°C and grease an Air fryer basket.
2. Mix all the ingredients in a large bowl except the chops.
3. Coat the pork chops with marinade generously and cover to refrigerate for about 3 hours.
4. Keep the pork chops at room temperature for about 30 minutes and transfer into the Air fryer basket.
5. Gill for about 12 minutes, flipping once in between and dish out to serve hot.

# Comforting Sausage Bake

PREP TIME: 15 minutes
COOK TIME: 30 minutes

**170 g plain flour**
**2 eggs**
**1 red onion, sliced thinly**
**175 ml milk**
**8 small sausages**
**What you'll need from the store cupboard:**
**15 ml olive oil**
**1 garlic clove, minced**
**Salt and black pepper, to taste**

1. Preheat the Air fryer to 160°C and grease a baking dish.
2. Sift the flour in a bowl and whisk in the eggs.
3. Combine well and add onion, garlic, milk, 155 ml cold water salt and black pepper.
4. Pierce 1 rosemary sprig in each sausage and transfer into the baking dish.
5. Top evenly with the flour mixture and air fry for about 30 minutes.
6. Dish out and serve warm.

# Ribs and Chimichurri Sauce

PREP TIME: 15 minutes
COOK TIME: 13 minutes

**455 g boneless short ribs**
**1½ tsps. sea salt, divided**
**1 tsp. minced garlic**
**1 tbsp. freshly squeezed lemon juice**
**½ tsp. ground cumin**
**½ tsp. freshly ground black pepper, divided**
**30 g fresh parsley leaves**
**30 g fresh coriander leaves**
**¼ tsp. red pepper flakes**
**2 tbsps. extra-virgin olive oil**
**Avocado oil spray**

1. Pat the short ribs dry with paper towels. Sprinkle the ribs all over with 1 tsp. salt and ¼ tsp. black pepper. Let it sit at room temperature for 45 minutes.
2. Meanwhile, place the parsley, coriander, garlic, lemon juice, cumin, red pepper flakes, the remaining ½ tsp. salt, and the remaining ¼ tsp. black pepper in a blender or food processor. With the blender running, slowly drizzle in the olive oil. Blend for about 1 minute, until the mixture is smooth and well combined.
3. Set the air fryer to 205°C. Spray both sides of the ribs with oil. Place in the basket and roast for 8 minutes. Flip and roast for another 5 minutes, until an instant-read thermometer reads 52°C for medium-rare (or to your desired doneness).
4. Allow the meat to rest for 5 to 10 minutes, then slice. Serve warm with the chimichurri sauce.

# Moist Stuffed Pork Roll

| PREP TIME: 20 minutes<br>COOK TIME: 15 minutes | 1 spring onion, chopped<br>15 g sun-dried tomatoes, chopped finely<br>2 tbsps. fresh parsley, chopped<br>4 (170 gram) pork cutlets, pounded slightly<br>**What you'll need from the store cupboard:**<br>½ tbsp. olive oil<br>Salt and black pepper, to taste<br>2 tsps. paprika |
|---|---|

1. Preheat the Air fryer to 200°C and grease an Air fryer basket.
2. Mix spring onion, tomatoes, parsley, salt and black pepper in a large bowl.
3. Coat the cutlets with tomato mixture and roll each cutlet.
4. Secure the cutlets with cocktail sticks and rub with paprika, salt and black pepper.
5. Coat evenly with oil and transfer into the Air fryer basket.
6. Roast for about 15 minutes, flipping once in between and dish out to serve hot.

# Pork and Lime Sauce

| PREP TIME: 10 minutes<br>COOK TIME: 15 minutes | **Marinade:**<br>120 ml lime juice<br>Grated zest of 1 lime<br>2 tsps. sweetener<br>3 cloves garlic, minced<br>1½ tsps. fine sea salt<br>1 tsp. chilli powder, or more for more heat<br>1 tsp. smoked paprika<br>455 g pork tenderloin<br>**Avocado Lime Sauce:**<br>1 medium-sized ripe avocado, roughly chopped<br>115 g full-fat sour cream<br>Grated zest of 1 lime<br>Juice of 1 lime<br>2 cloves garlic, roughly chopped<br>½ tsp. fine sea salt<br>¼ tsp. ground black pepper<br>Chopped fresh coriander leaves, for garnish<br>Lime slices, for serving<br>Pico de gallo, for serving |
|---|---|

1. In a medium-sized casserole dish, stir together all the marinade ingredients until well combined. Add the tenderloin and coat it well in the marinade. Cover and place in the fridge to marinate for 2 hours or overnight.
2. Spray the air fryer basket with avocado oil. Preheat the air fryer to 205°C.
3. Remove the pork from the marinade and place it in the air fryer basket. Roast for 13 to 15 minutes, until the internal temperature of the pork is 60°C, flipping after 7 minutes. Remove the pork from the air fryer and place it on a cutting board. Allow it to rest for 8 to 10 minutes, then cut it into 1-cm thick slices.
4. While the pork cooks, make the avocado lime sauce: Place all the sauce ingredients in a food processor and purée until smooth. Taste and adjust the seasoning to your liking.
5. Place the pork slices on a serving platter and spoon the avocado lime sauce on top. Garnish with coriander leaves and serve with lime slices and pico de gallo.
6. Store leftovers in an airtight container in the fridge for up to 4 days. Reheat in a preheated 205°C air fryer for 5 minutes, or until heated through.

# Pork Meatballs and Worcester Sauce

**SERVES 4**

| | |
|---|---|
| PREP TIME: 20 minutes<br>COOK TIME: 15 minutes | 1½ tbsps. Worcester sauce<br>1 tbsp. coconut aminos<br>1 tsp. turmeric powder<br>½ tsp. freshly grated ginger root<br>1 small sliced red chilli, for garnish<br>455 g pork mince<br>60 g spring onions, finely chopped<br>2 cloves garlic, finely minced |

1. Mix all of the above ingredients, apart from the red chilli. Knead with your hands to ensure an even mixture.
2. Roll into equal balls and transfer them to the Air Fryer cooking basket.
3. Set the timer for 15 minutes and push the power button. Air-fry at 180°C. Sprinkle with sliced red chilli, serve immediately with your favorite sauce for dipping. Enjoy!

# Flavoursome Pork Chops and Peanut Sauce

**SERVES 4**

| | |
|---|---|
| PREP TIME: 30 minutes<br>COOK TIME: 21 minutes | 450 g pork chops, cubed into 2.5-centimetre size<br>1 shallot, chopped finely<br>180 g peanut butter<br>175 ml coconut milk<br>What you'll need from the store cupboard:<br>For Pork:<br>1 tsp. fresh ginger, minced<br>1 garlic clove, minced<br>30 ml soy sauce<br>15 ml olive oil<br>1 tsp. hot pepper sauce<br>For Peanut Sauce:<br>15 ml olive oil<br>1 tsp. hot pepper sauce<br>15 ml olive oil<br>1 garlic clove, minced<br>1 tsp. ground coriander |

1. Preheat the Air fryer to 200°C and grease an Air fryer basket.
2. For Pork:
3. Mix all the ingredients in a bowl and keep aside for about 30 minutes.
4. Arrange the chops in the Air fryer basket and roast for about 12 minutes, flipping once in between.
5. For Peanut Sauce:
6. Heat olive oil in a pan on medium heat and add shallot and garlic.
7. Sauté for about 3 minutes and stir in coriander.
8. Sauté for about 1 minute and add rest of the ingredients.
9. Roast for about 5 minutes and pour over the pork chops to serve.

# CHAPTER 8
# LAMB

# Mustard Lamb Loin Chops

**PREP TIME:** 15 minutes
**COOK TIME:** 30 minutes

8 (115 gram) lamb loin chops
**What you'll need from the store cupboard:**
**2 tbsps. Dijon mustard**
**15 ml fresh lemon juice**
**½ tsp. olive oil**
**1 tsp. dried tarragon**
**Salt and black pepper, to taste**

1. Preheat the Air fryer to 200°C and grease an Air fryer basket.
2. Mix the mustard, lemon juice, oil, tarragon, salt, and black pepper in a large bowl.
3. Coat the chops generously with the mustard mixture and arrange in the Air fryer basket.
4. Grill for about 15 minutes, flipping once in between and dish out to serve hot.

# Spiced Lamb Steaks

**PREP TIME:** 15 minutes
**COOK TIME:** 15 minutes

**½ onion, roughly chopped**
**680 g boneless lamb sirloin steaks**
**What you'll need from the store cupboard:**
**½ tsp. ground cumin**
**½ tsp. ground cinnamon**
**½ tsp. cayenne pepper**
**5 garlic cloves, peeled**
**1 tbsp. fresh ginger, peeled**
**1 tsp. garam masala**
**1 tsp. ground fennel**
**Salt and black pepper, to taste**

1. Preheat the Air fryer to 165°C and grease an Air fryer basket.
2. Put the onion, garlic, ginger, and spices in a blender and pulse until smooth.
3. Coat the lamb steaks with this mixture on both sides and refrigerate to marinate for about 24 hours.
4. Arrange the lamb steaks in the Air fryer basket and roast for about 15 minutes, flipping once in between.
5. Dish out the steaks in a platter and serve warm.

# Lime Marinated Lamb Chop

**PREP TIME:** 5 minutes
**COOK TIME:** 5 minutes

**2 (2-cm thick) lamb chops**
**Sprigs of fresh mint, for garnish (optional)**
**Lime slices, for serving (optional)**
**Marinade:**
**4 cloves garlic, roughly chopped**
**2 tsps. fine sea salt**
**½ tsp. ground black pepper**
**2 tsps. grated lime zest**
**120 ml lime juice**
**60 ml avocado oil**
**15 g chopped fresh mint leaves**

1. Make the marinade: Place all the ingredients for the marinade in a food processor or blender and purée until mostly smooth with a few small chunks. Transfer half of the marinade to a shallow dish and set the other half aside for serving. Add the lamb to the shallow dish, cover, and place in the refrigerator to marinate for at least 2 hours or overnight.
2. Spray the air fryer basket with avocado oil. Preheat the air fryer to 200°C.
3. Remove the chops from the marinade and place them in the air fryer basket. Roast for 5 minutes, or until the internal temperature reaches 60°C for medium doneness.
4. Allow the chops to rest for 10 minutes before serving with the rest of the marinade as a sauce. Garnish with fresh mint leaves and serve with lime slices, if desired. Best served fresh.

# Fast Lamb Satay

**PREP TIME:** 5 minutes
**COOK TIME:** 8 minutes

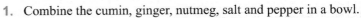

**¼ tsp. cumin**
**2 boneless lamb steaks**
**Cooking spray**
**1 tsp. ginger**
**½ tsps. nutmeg**
**Salt and ground black pepper, to taste**

1. Combine the cumin, ginger, nutmeg, salt and pepper in a bowl.
2. Cube the lamb steaks and massage the spice mixture into each one.
3. Leave to marinate for 10 minutes, then transfer onto metal skewers.
4. Preheat the air fryer to 200°C.
5. Spritz the skewers with the cooking spray, then air fry them in the air fryer for 8 minutes.
6. Take care when removing them from the air fryer and serve.

# Herbed Lamb Chops

**SERVES 2**

**PREP TIME:** 10 minutes
**COOK TIME:** 15 minutes

**4 (115 gram) lamb chops**
**What you'll need from the store cupboard:**
**1 tsp. dried rosemary**
**1 tsp. dried thyme**
**1 tsp. dried oregano**
**15 ml fresh lemon juice**
**15 ml olive oil**
**½ tsp. ground cumin**
**½ tsp. ground coriander**
**Salt and black pepper, to taste**

1. Preheat the Air fryer to 200°C and grease an Air fryer basket.
2. Mix the lemon juice, oil, herbs, and spices in a large bowl.
3. Coat the chops generously with the herb mixture and refrigerate to marinate for about 1 hour.
4. Arrange the chops in the Air fryer basket and roast for about 15 minutes, flipping once in between.
5. Dish out the lamb chops in a platter and serve hot.

# Roasted Lamb

**SERVES 4**

**PREP TIME:** 15 minutes
**COOK TIME:** 1 hour 30 minutes

**1 tbsp. dried rosemary**
**15 ml olive oil**
**1¼-kilogram half lamb leg roast, slits carved**
**2 garlic cloves, sliced into smaller slithers**
**What you'll need from the store cupboard:**
**Cracked Himalayan rock salt and cracked peppercorns, to taste**

1. Preheat the Air fryer to 200°C and grease an Air fryer basket.
2. Insert the garlic slithers in the slits and brush with rosemary, oil, salt, and black pepper.
3. Arrange the lamb in the Air fryer basket and roast for about 15 minutes.
4. Set the Air fryer to 175°C on the Roast mode and roast for 1 hour and 15 minutes.
5. Dish out the lamb and serve hot.

# Lamb Meatballs

PREP TIME: 20 minutes
COOK TIME: 8 minutes

**Meatballs:**
2 tsps. fresh oregano, finely chopped
2 tbsps. milk
1 egg yolk
½ small onion, finely diced
1 clove garlic, minced
454 g lamb mince
2 tbsps. fresh parsley, finely chopped (plus more for garnish)
Salt and freshly ground black pepper, to taste

80 g crumbled feta cheese, for garnish
**Tomato Sauce:**
2 tbsps. butter
1 clove garlic, smashed
Pinch crushed red pepper flakes
¼ tsp. ground cinnamon
1 (794-g) tin crushed tomatoes
Salt, to taste
Olive oil, for greasing

1. Combine all ingredients for the meatballs in a large bowl and mix just until everything is combined. Shape the mixture into 3-cm balls or shape the meat between two spoons to make quenelles.
2. Preheat the air fryer to 200°C.
3. While the air fryer is preheating, start the quick tomato sauce. Put the butter, garlic and red pepper flakes in a sauté pan and heat over medium heat on the stovetop. Let the garlic sizzle a little, but before the butter browns, add the cinnamon and tomatoes. Bring to a simmer and simmer for 15 minutes. Season with salt.
4. Grease the bottom of the air fryer basket with olive oil and transfer the meatballs to the air fryer basket in one layer, air frying in batches if necessary.
5. Air fry for 8 minutes, giving the basket a shake once during the cooking process to turn the meatballs over.
6. To serve, spoon a pool of the tomato sauce onto plates and add the meatballs. Sprinkle the feta cheese on top and garnish with more fresh parsley. Serve immediately.

# Lamb Leg with Brussels Sprouts

PREP TIME: 20 minutes
COOK TIME: 1 hour 30 minutes

1 kilogram leg of lamb
1 tbsp. fresh rosemary, minced
1 tbsp. fresh lemon thyme
680 g Brussels sprouts, trimmed
**What you'll need from the store cupboard:**
Salt and ground black pepper, as required
40 g honey
45 ml olive oil, divided
1 garlic clove, minced

1. Preheat the Air fryer to 150°C and grease an Air fryer basket.
2. Make slits in the leg of lamb with a sharp knife.
3. Mix 30 ml of oil, herbs, garlic, salt, and black pepper in a bowl.
4. Coat the leg of lamb with oil mixture generously and arrange in the Air fryer basket.
5. Roast for about 75 minutes and set the Air fryer to 200 o F.
6. Coat the Brussels sprout evenly with the remaining oil and honey and arrange them in the Air fryer basket with leg of lamb.
7. Roast for about 15 minutes and dish out to serve warm.

# Pesto Coated Lamb Rack

**SERVES 4**

PREP TIME: 15 minutes
COOK TIME: 15 minutes

½ bunch fresh mint
1 (680 gram) rack of lamb
What you'll need from the store cupboard:
10 g honey
1 garlic clove
60 ml extra-virgin olive oil
Salt and black pepper, to taste

1. Preheat the Air fryer to 200°C and grease an Air fryer basket.
2. Put the mint, garlic, oil, honey, salt, and black pepper in a blender and pulse until smooth to make pesto.
3. Coat the rack of lamb with this pesto on both sides and arrange in the Air fryer basket.
4. Roast for about 15 minutes and cut the rack into individual chops to serve.

# Lollipop Lamb Chops

**SERVES 4**

PREP TIME: 15 minutes
COOK TIME: 7 minutes

8 lamb chops (1 rack)
½ small clove garlic
15 g packed fresh parsley
50 g packed fresh mint
½ tsp. lemon juice
22 g grated Parmesan cheese
50 g shelled pistachios
¼ tsp. salt
120 ml olive oil
2 tbsps. vegetable oil
Salt and freshly ground black pepper, to taste
1 tbsp. dried rosemary, chopped
1 tbsp. dried thyme

1. Make the pesto by combining the garlic, parsley and mint in a food processor and process until finely chopped. Add the lemon juice, Parmesan cheese, pistachios and salt. Process until all the ingredients have turned into a paste. With the processor running, slowly pour the olive oil in. Scrape the sides of the processor with a spatula and process for another 30 seconds.
2. Preheat the air fryer to 200°C.
3. Rub both sides of the lamb chops with vegetable oil and season with salt, pepper, rosemary and thyme, pressing the herbs into the meat gently with the fingers. Transfer the lamb chops to the air fryer basket.
4. Air fry the lamb chops for 5 minutes. Flip the chops over and air fry for an additional 2 minutes.
5. Serve the lamb chops with mint pesto drizzled on top.

# Air Fried Lamb Ribs

**PREP TIME:** 5 minutes
**COOK TIME:** 18 minutes

2 tbsps. mustard
15 g mint leaves, chopped
280 g Greek yoghurt
454 g lamb ribs
1 tsp. rosemary, chopped
Salt and ground black pepper, to taste

1. Preheat the air fryer to 180°C.
2. Use a brush to apply the mustard to the lamb ribs, and season with rosemary, salt, and pepper.
3. Air fry the ribs in the air fryer for 18 minutes.
4. Meanwhile, combine the mint leaves and yoghurt in a bowl.
5. Remove the lamb ribs from the air fryer when cooked and serve with the mint yoghurt.

# Herbed Lamb Chops with Parmesan

SERVES 2

**PREP TIME:** 10 minutes
**COOK TIME:** 5 minutes

1 large egg
2 cloves garlic, minced
25 g powdered Parmesan cheese
1 tbsp. chopped fresh oregano leaves
1 tbsp. chopped fresh rosemary leaves
1 tsp. chopped fresh thyme leaves
½ tsp. ground black pepper
4 (2-cm-thick) lamb chops
For Garnish/Serving (Optional):
Lavender flowers
Lemon slices
Sprigs of fresh oregano
Sprigs of fresh rosemary
Sprigs of fresh thyme

1. Spray the air fryer basket with avocado oil. Preheat the air fryer to 205°C..
2. Beat the egg in a shallow bowl, add the garlic, and stir well to combine. In another shallow bowl, mix together Parmesan, herbs, and pepper.
3. One at a time, dip the lamb chops into the egg mixture, shake off the excess egg, and then dredge them in the Parmesan mixture. Use your hands to coat the chops well in the Parmesan mixture and form a nice crust on all sides, if necessary, dip the chops again in both the egg and the Parmesan mixture.
4. Place the lamb chops in the air fryer basket, leaving space between them, and roast for 5 minutes, or until the internal temperature reaches 60°C for medium doneness. Allow them to rest for 10 minutes before serving.
5. Garnish with sprigs of oregano, rosemary, and thyme, and lavender flowers, if desired. Serve with lemon slices, if desired.
6. Best served fresh. Store leftovers in an airtight container in the fridge for up to 4 days. Serve chilled over a salad, or reheat in a 175°C air fryer for 3 minutes, or until heated through.

\

# Simple Lamb Chops

PREP TIME: 10 minutes
COOK TIME: 15 minutes

Salt and black pepper, to taste
15 ml olive oil
4 (115 gram) lamb chops
What you'll need from the store cupboard:

1. Preheat the Air fryer to 200°C and grease an Air fryer basket.
2. Mix the olive oil, salt, and black pepper in a large bowl and add chops.
3. Arrange the chops in the Air fryer basket and roast for about 15 minutes.
4. Dish out the lamb chops and serve hot.

# Za'atar Lamb Loin Chops

PREP TIME: 10 minutes
COOK TIME: 15 minutes

8 (100 gram) bone-in lamb loin chops, trimmed
What you'll need from the store cupboard:
3 garlic cloves, crushed
15 ml fresh lemon juice
5 ml olive oil
1 tbsp. Za'atar
Salt and black pepper, to taste

1. Preheat the Air fryer to 200°C and grease an Air fryer basket.
2. Mix the garlic, lemon juice, oil, Za'atar, salt, and black pepper in a large bowl.
3. Coat the chops generously with the herb mixture and arrange the chops in the Air fryer basket.
4. Roast for about 15 minutes, flipping twice in between and dish out the lamb chops to serve hot.
5. Nutrition Facts Per Serving:
6. Calories: 433, Fat: 17.6g, Carbohydrates: 0.6g, Sugar: 0.2g, Protein: 64.1g, Sodium: 201mg

(Note: Za'atar - Za'atar is generally made with ground dried thyme, oregano, marjoram, or some combination thereof, mixed with toasted sesame seeds, and salt, though other spices such as sumac might also be added. Some commercial varieties also include roasted flour.)

# CHAPTER 9
# SNACK

# Crispy Spiced Chickpeas

**MAKES 1½ CUPS**

PREP TIME: 5 minutes
COOK TIME: 6 to 12 minutes

½ tsp. dried chives
¼ tsp. mustard powder
¼ tsp. sweet paprika
¼ tsp. cayenne pepper
1 tin (420-g) chickpeas, rinsed and dried with paper towels
1 tbsp. olive oil
½ tsp. dried rosemary
½ tsp. dried parsley
Salt and freshly ground black pepper, to taste

1.  Preheat the air fryer to 180ºC.
2.  In a large bowl, combine all the ingredients, except for the salt and black pepper, and toss until the chickpeas are evenly coated in the herbs and spices.
3.  Scrape the chickpeas and seasonings into the air fryer and air fry for 6 to 12 minutes, or until browned and crisp, shaking the basket half-way through.
4.  Transfer the crispy chickpeas to a bowl, sprinkle with salt and black pepper, and serve warm.

# Lemony Pear Crisps

**SERVES 4**

PREP TIME: 15 minutes
COOK TIME: 9 to 13 minutes

½ tsp. ground cinnamon
⅛ tsp. ground cardamom
2 firm Bosc pears, cut crosswise into ¼ -cm-thick slices
1 tbsp. freshly squeezed lemon juice

1.  Preheat the air fryer to 190ºC.
2.  Separate the smaller stem-end pear rounds from the larger rounds with seeds. Remove the core and seeds from the larger slices. Sprinkle all slices with lemon juice, cinnamon, and cardamom.
3.  Put the smaller crisps into the air fryer basket. Air fry for 3 to 5 minutes, or until light golden brown, shaking the basket once during cooking. Remove from the air fryer.
4.  Repeat with the larger slices, air frying for 6 to 8 minutes, or until light golden brown, shaking the basket once during cooking.
5.  Remove the crisps from the air fryer. Cool and serve or store in an airtight container at room temperature up for to 2 days.

# Spiced Mixed Nuts

PREP TIME: 5 minutes
COOK TIME: 6 minutes

½ tsp. ground coriander
¼ tsp. onion powder
¼ tsp. freshly ground black pepper
⅛ tsp. garlic powder
75 g raw cashews
75 g raw pecan halves
75 g raw walnut halves
75 g raw whole almonds
2 tbsps. olive oil
1 tbsp. light brown sugar
1 tsp. chopped fresh rosemary leaves
1 tsp. chopped fresh thyme leaves
1 tsp. salt

1. Preheat the air fryer to 180ºC.
2. In a large bowl, combine all the ingredients and toss until the nuts are evenly coated in the herbs, spices, and sugar.
3. Scrape the nuts and seasonings into the air fryer and air fry for 6 minutes, or until golden brown and fragrant, shaking the basket halfway through.
4. Transfer the cocktail nuts to a bowl and serve warm.

# Bacon-Wrapped Prawns with Red Chilli

PREP TIME: 20 minutes
COOK TIME: 26 minutes

12 strips bacon, cut in half
24 small pickled red chilli slices
24 large prawns, peeled and deveined, about 340 g
5 tbsps. barbecue sauce, divided

1. Toss together the prawns and 3 tbsps. of the barbecue sauce. Let stand for 15 minutes. Soak 24 wooden toothpicks in water for 10 minutes. Wrap 1 piece bacon around the prawn and red chilli slice, then secure with a toothpick.
2. Preheat the air fryer to 180ºC.
3. Working in batches, place half of the prawns in the air fryer basket, spacing them 1-cm apart. Air fry for 10 minutes. Turn prawns over with tongs and air fry for 3 minutes more, or until bacon is golden brown and prawns are cooked through.
4. Brush with the remaining barbecue sauce and serve.

# Cheesy Stuffed Mushrooms

PREP TIME: 10 minutes
COOK TIME: 8 to 12 minutes

⅛ tsp. cayenne pepper
3 tbsps. shredded Pepper Jack cheese
2 tsps. olive oil
16 medium button mushrooms, rinsed and patted dry
70 g low-sodium salsa
3 garlic cloves, minced
1 medium onion, finely chopped
1 red chilli, minced

1. Preheat the air fryer to 180°C.
2. Remove the stems from the mushrooms and finely chop them, reserving the whole caps.
3. In a medium bowl, mix the salsa, garlic, onion, red chilli, cayenne, and Pepper Jack cheese. Stir in the chopped mushroom stems.
4. Stuff this mixture into the mushroom caps, mounding the filling. Drizzle the olive oil on the mushrooms. Air fry the mushrooms in the air fryer basket for 8 to 12 minutes, or until the filling is hot and the mushrooms are tender.
5. Serve immediately.

# Spiced Sweet Potato Fries

PREP TIME: 10 minutes
COOK TIME: 15 minutes

½ tsp. ground turmeric
½ tsp. mustard powder
¼ tsp. cayenne pepper
1½ tsps. smoked paprika
1½ tsps. salt, plus more as needed
1 tsp. chilli powder
½ tsp. ground cumin
2 tbsps. olive oil
2 medium sweet potatoes (about 284 g each), cut into wedges, 1-cm thick and 6-cm long
Freshly ground black pepper, to taste
150 g sour cream
1 garlic clove, grated

1. Preheat the air fryer to 200°C.
2. In a large bowl, combine the olive oil, paprika, salt, chilli powder, cumin, turmeric, mustard powder, and cayenne. Add the sweet potatoes, season with black pepper, and toss to evenly coat.
3. Transfer the sweet potatoes to the air fryer (save the bowl with the leftover oil and spices) and air fry for 15 minutes, shaking the basket halfway through, or until golden brown and crisp. Return the potato wedges to the reserved bowl and toss again while they are hot.
4. Meanwhile, in a small bowl, stir together the sour cream and garlic. Season with salt and black pepper and transfer to a serving dish.
5. Serve the potato wedges hot with the garlic sour cream.

# Coconut-Crusted Prawns

**PREP TIME:** 10 minutes
**COOK TIME:** 4 minutes

**220 g medium prawns, peeled and deveined (tails intact)**
**240 ml canned coconut milk**
**60 g panko bread crumbs**
**40 g unsweetened desiccated Coconut**
**Freshly ground black pepper, to taste**
**Finely grated zest of 1 lime**
**salt, to taste**
**Cooking spray**
**1 small or ½ medium cucumber, halved and deseeded**
**250 g coconut yoghurt**
**1 serrano chilli, deseeded and minced**

1. Preheat the air fryer to 200ºC.
2. In a bowl, combine the prawns, coconut milk, lime zest, and ½ tsp. salt. Let the prawns stand for 10 minutes.
3. Meanwhile, in a separate bowl, stir together the bread crumbs and desiccated Coconut and season with salt and pepper.
4. A few at a time, add the prawns to the bread crumb mixture and toss to coat completely. Transfer the prawns to a wire rack set over a baking sheet. Spray the prawns all over with cooking spray.
5. Transfer the prawns to the air fryer and air fry for 4 minutes, or until golden brown and cooked through. Transfer the prawns to a serving platter and season with more salt.
6. Grate the cucumber into a small bowl. Stir in the coconut yoghurt and chilli and season with salt and pepper. Serve alongside the prawns while they're warm.

# Crispy Apple Crisps

**PREP TIME:** 5 minutes
**COOK TIME:** 25 to 35 minutes

**1 Honeycrisp or Pink Lady apple**

1. Preheat the air fryer to 150ºC.
2. Core the apple with an apple corer, leaving apple whole. Cut the apple into ¼-cm-thick slices.
3. Arrange the apple slices in the basket, staggering slices as much as possible. Air fry for 25 to 35 minutes, or until the crisps are dry and some are lightly browned, turning 4 times with tongs to separate and rotate them from top to bottom.
4. Place the crisps in a single layer on a wire rack to cool. Apples will become crisper as they cool. Serve immediately.

# Buffalo Cauliflower and Sour Dip

**SERVES 6**

**PREP TIME:** 10 minutes
**COOK TIME:** 10 to 14 minutes

½ tsps. Tabasco sauce
1 celery stick, chopped
1 tbsp. crumbled blue cheese
1 large head cauliflower, separated into small florets
1 tbsp. olive oil
½ tsp. garlic powder
70 g low-sodium hot wing sauce, divided
170 g nonfat Greek yoghurt

1. Preheat the air fryer to 190ºC.
2. In a large bowl, toss the cauliflower florets with the olive oil. Sprinkle with the garlic powder and toss again to coat. Put half of the cauliflower in the air fryer basket. Air fry for 5 to 7 minutes, or until the cauliflower is browned, shaking the basket once during cooking.
3. Transfer to a serving bowl and toss with half of the wing sauce. Repeat with the remaining cauliflower and wing sauce.
4. In a small bowl, stir together the yoghurt, Tabasco sauce, celery, and blue cheese. Serve the cauliflower with the dip.

# Peppery Chicken Meatballs

**MAKES 16 MEATBALLS**

**PREP TIME:** 5 minutes
**COOK TIME:** 13 to 20 minutes

1 egg white
½ tsp. dried thyme
220 g chicken breast mince
2 tsps. olive oil
15 g minced onion
20 g minced red pepper
2 vanilla wafers, crushed

1. Preheat the air fryer to 190ºC.
2. In a baking pan, mix the olive oil, onion, and red pepper. Put the pan in the air fryer. Air fry for 3 to 5 minutes, or until the vegetables are tender.
3. In a medium bowl, mix the cooked vegetables, crushed wafers, egg white, and thyme until well combined
4. Mix in the chicken, gently but thoroughly, until everything is combined.
5. Form the mixture into 16 meatballs and place them in the air fryer basket. Air fry for 10 to 15 minutes, or until the meatballs reach an internal temperature of 75ºC on a meat thermometer.
6. Serve immediately.

# Rosemary-Garlic Shoestring Fries

**SERVES 2**

**PREP TIME:** 5 minutes
**COOK TIME:** 18 minutes

1 large russet potato (340 g), scrubbed clean, and julienned
1 tbsp. vegetable oil
1 garlic clove, thinly sliced
Flaky sea salt, for serving
Leaves from 1 sprig fresh rosemary
Salt and freshly ground black pepper, to taste

1. Preheat the air fryer to 200ºC.
2. Place the julienned potatoes in a large colander and rinse under cold running water until the water runs clear. Spread the potatoes out on a double-thick layer of paper towels and pat dry.
3. In a large bowl, combine the potatoes, oil, and rosemary. Season with salt and pepper and toss to coat evenly. Place the potatoes in the air fryer and air fry for 18 minutes, shaking the basket every 5 minutes and adding the garlic in the last 5 minutes of cooking, or until the fries are golden brown and crisp.
4. Transfer the fries to a plate and sprinkle with flaky sea salt while they're hot. Serve immediately.


# Baked Ricotta

**MAKES 2 CUPS**

**PREP TIME:** 10 minutes
**COOK TIME:** 15 minutes

¼ tsp. salt
¼ tsp. pepper
1 (420-g) container whole milk Ricotta cheese
3 tbsps. grated Parmesan cheese, divided
2 tbsps. extra-virgin olive oil
1 tsp. chopped fresh thyme leaves
1 tsp. grated lemon zest
1 clove garlic, crushed with press
Toasted baguette slices or crackers, for serving

1. Preheat the air fryer to 190ºC.
2. To get the baking dish in and out of the air fryer, create a sling using a 48-cm length of foil, folded lengthwise into thirds.
3. Whisk together the Ricotta, 2 tbsps. of the Parmesan, oil, thyme, lemon zest, garlic, salt, and pepper. Pour into a baking dish. Cover the dish tightly with foil.
4. Place the sling under dish and lift by the ends into the air fryer, tucking the ends of the sling around the dish. Bake for 10 minutes. Remove the foil cover and sprinkle with the remaining 1 tbsp. of the Parmesan. Air fry for 5 more minutes, or until bubbly at edges and the top is browned.
5. Serve warm with toasted baguette slices or crackers.

# Veggie Prawn Toast

PREP TIME: 15 minutes
COOK TIME: 3 to 6 minutes

8 large raw prawns, peeled and finely chopped
1 egg white
1 medium celery stick, minced
2 tbsps. cornflour
2 garlic cloves, minced
3 tbsps. minced red pepper
¼ tsp. Chinese five-spice powder
3 slices firm thin-sliced no-sodium whole-wheat bread

1. Preheat the air fryer to 180ºC.
2. In a small bowl, stir together the prawns, egg white, garlic, red pepper, celery, cornflour, and five-spice powder. Top each slice of bread with one-third of the prawn mixture, spreading it evenly to the edges. With a sharp knife, cut each slice of bread into 4 strips.
3. Place the prawn toasts in the air fryer basket in a single layer. You may need to cook them in batches. Air fry for 3 to 6 minutes, until crisp and golden brown.
4. Serve hot.

# Creamy Spinach-Broccoli Dip

SERVES 4

PREP TIME: 10 minutes
COOK TIME: 9 to 14 minutes

1 garlic clove, minced
½ tsp. dried oregano
140 g low-fat Greek yoghurt
50 g nonfat cream cheese
35 g frozen chopped broccoli, thawed and drained
20 g frozen chopped spinach, thawed and drained
40 g chopped red pepper
2 tbsps. grated low-sodium Parmesan cheese

1. Preheat the air fryer to 170ºC.
2. In a medium bowl, blend the yoghurt and cream cheese until well combined.
3. Stir in the broccoli, spinach, red pepper, garlic, and oregano. Transfer to a baking pan. Sprinkle with the Parmesan cheese.
4. Place the pan in the air fryer basket. Bake for 9 to 14 minutes, or until the dip is bubbly and the top starts to brown.
5. Serve immediately.

# APPENDIX 1:
# RECIPES INDEX

# APPENDIX 2:
# AIR FRY COOKING TIME CHART

| INGREDIENT | AMOUNT | PREPARATION | TOSS IN OIL | TEMP | COOK TIME |
|---|---|---|---|---|---|
| **VEGETABLES** | | | | | |
| Broccoli | ½ head | Cut in 1-inch florets | 1 tbsp. | 400°F | 15–18 mins |
| Cauliflower | ½ head | Cut in 1-inch florets | 1 tbsp. | 400°F | 20–25 mins |
| Potatoes, russet | 2 small | Cut in 1-inch wedges | 1 tbsp. | 400°F | 25–30 mins |
| | 1 whole (6–8 oz) | Pierced with fork 3 times | None | 400°F | 35–40 mins |
| **POULTRY** | | | | | |
| Chicken breasts | 1 breast (6–8 oz each) | Boneless | Brushed with oil | 400°F | 20–24 mins |
| Chicken wings | ¾ lb. (12 oz) | Drumettes & flats | None | 400°F | 22–26 mins |
| **FISH & SEAFOOD** | | | | | |
| Salmon fillets | 2 fillets (4 oz each) | None | Brushed with oil | 400°F | 10–13 mins |
| **PORK** | | | | | |
| Hot Dogs | 4 hot dogs | Whole | None | 400°F | 8–10 mins |
| **FROZEN FOODS** | | | | | |
| Burger, frozen | ¼ lb. patty | 1 inch thick | None | 400°F | 10–15 mins |
| Chicken nuggets | 1 box (12 oz) | None | None | 400°F | 13–15 mins |
| Fish sticks | 8 fish sticks | None | None | 400°F | 10–15 mins |
| French fries | ½ lb. | None | None | 400°F | 18–23 mins |
| Mozzarella sticks | ½ box (8 oz) | None | None | 400°F | 12–15 mins |
| Pot stickers | ½ bag (12 oz, 10 count) | None | None | 400°F | 12–15 mins |
| Pizza rolls | ½ bag (10 oz, 20 count) | None | None | 400°F | 12–15 mins |
| Popcorn shrimp | 1 box (14–16 ounces) | None | None | 400°F | 12–15 mins |
| Frozen sweet potato fries | ½ bag (10 oz) | None | None | 400°F | 20–22 mins |
| Tater tots | ½ lb. | None | None | 400°F | 20–22 mins |

# APPENDIX 3:
# BASIC KITCHEN CONVERSIONS & EQUIVALENTS

## DRY MEASUREMENTS CONVERSION CHART
3 teaspoons = 1 tablespoon = 1/16 cup
6 teaspoons = 2 tablespoons = 1/8 cup
12 teaspoons = 4 tablespoons = ¼ cup
24 teaspoons = 8 tablespoons = ½ cup
36 teaspoons = 12 tablespoons = ¾ cup
48 teaspoons = 16 tablespoons = 1 cup

## *METRIC TO US COOKING CONVERSIONS*

### OVEN TEMPERATURES
120 °C = 250 °F
160 °C = 320 °F
180 °C = 350 °F
205 °C = 400 °F
220 °C = 425 °F

### LIQUID MEASUREMENTS CONVERSION CHART
8 fluid ounces = 1 cup = ½ pint = ¼ quart
16 fluid ounces = 2 cups = 1 pint = ½ quart
32 fluid ounces = 4 cups = 2 pints = 1 quart = ¼ gallon
128 fluid ounces = 16 cups = 8 pints = 4 quarts = 1 gallon

### BAKING IN GRAMS
1 cup flour = 140 grams
1 cup sugar = 150 grams
1 cup powdered sugar = 160 grams
1 cup heavy cream = 235 grams

### VOLUME
1 milliliter = 1/5 teaspoon
5 ml = 1 teaspoon
15 ml = 1 tablespoon
240 ml = 1 cup or 8 fluid ounces
1 liter = 34 fluid ounces

### WEIGHT
1 gram = .035 ounces
100 grams = 3.5 ounces
500 grams = 1.1 pounds
1 kilogram = 35 ounces

## *US TO METRIC COOKING CONVERSIONS*

1/5 tsp = 1 ml
1 tsp = 5 ml
1 tbsp = 15 ml
1 fluid ounces = 30 ml
1 cup = 237 ml
1 pint (2 cups) = 473 ml
1 quart (4 cups) = .95 liter
1 gallon (16 cups) = 3.8 liters
1 oz = 28 grams
1 pound = 454 grams

### BUTTER
1 cup butter = 2 sticks = 8 ounces = 230 grams = 16 tablespoons

### WHAT DOES 1 CUP EQUAL
1 cup = 8 fluid ounces
1 cup = 16 tablespoons
1 cup = 48 teaspoons
1 cup = ½ pint
1 cup = ¼ quart
1 cup = 1/16 gallon
1 cup = 240 ml

### BAKING PAN CONVERSIONS
9-inch round cake pan = 12 cups
10-inch tube pan =16 cups
10-inch bundt pan = 12 cups
9-inch springform pan = 10 cups
9 x 5 inch loaf pan = 8 cups
9-inch square pan = 8 cups

### BAKING PAN CONVERSIONS
1 cup all-purpose flour = 4.5 oz
1 cup rolled oats = 3 oz
1 large egg = 1.7 oz
1 cup butter = 8 oz
1 cup milk = 8 oz
1 cup heavy cream = 8.4 oz
1 cup granulated sugar = 7.1 oz
1 cup packed brown sugar = 7.75 oz
1 cup vegetable oil = 7.7 oz
1 cup unsifted powdered sugar = 4.4 oz

Printed in Great Britain
by Amazon

36819844R00044